I0473558

WHEN WORK DISAPPEARS

Rebuilding confidence, structure, and direction after work ends

Dave Cook

Yorkshire Cowboy Ltd

Printed in the United Kingdom.

For more information, contact:
dave@yorkshirecowboy.com
https://www.yorkshirecowboy.com

Book design by Dave Cook
Cover design by Dave Cook

ISBN - Paperback: 978-1-0686549-7-8

First Edition: March 2026

Dedication

For anyone finding their footing
when work ends.

Foreword

Work has disappeared for me four times in my career.

Each time was different. Different roles, different circumstances, different stages of life. And yet, each time unsettled me in familiar ways. The practical implications were obvious enough, income, routine, plans put on hold. What caught me off guard, repeatedly, was everything else.

When work disappears, it doesn't do so cleanly. It takes with it structure. It loosens identity. It distorts how you think about yourself and your value. Even when you know, rationally, that roles end for many reasons, the experience can still feel personal. Confidence wobbles. Perspective narrows. Time starts to behave strangely.

I didn't lack resilience or experience. I wasn't new to responsibility or uncertainty. And yet, each time work ended, I found myself grappling with the same quiet questions:

- What does this say about me?
- How long should this take?
- What should I be doing right now?

Those questions rarely arrived politely. They came with urgency, self-criticism, and the sense that I ought to be handling things better than I was.

Looking back, I don't think what I needed in those moments was motivation or reassurance. I didn't need to be told to "stay positive" or to treat the situation as an opportunity. And I'm not convinced that having a perfectly formed plan would have helped either.

What I needed was perspective. I needed someone to tell me that the confusion I was experiencing was normal. That the loss of structure would take time to recalibrate. That confidence would ebb before it returned. That uncertainty didn't mean I was broken or behind.

Most of all, I needed language. Language to describe what was happening without turning it into a problem to solve immediately. Language that allowed me to be unfinished without feeling diminished by it. Language that didn't force me to explain myself before I understood my own situation.

This book contains the advice I wish I'd had then.

Not advice that would have magically reduced my stress levels. Those moments were stressful, and some of that was unavoidable. But it would have given me a better understanding of what was happening beneath the surface, and how best to proceed without rushing myself or making things harder than they needed to be.

It would have helped me recognise that progress doesn't always look like forward motion. That steadiness matters more than speed. That clarity often arrives after movement has already begun, sometimes quietly, sometimes in hindsight.

Over time, and through repeated experience, I learned many of these lessons the hard way. This book is an attempt to make them available sooner to others who find themselves in a similar position.

It isn't a job-search manual. It isn't a productivity guide. It doesn't promise answers, certainty, or quick resolution. What it offers instead is orientation. A way to make sense of the in-between, when familiar markers of success no longer apply and the pressure to "do something" can become overwhelming.

If you are reading this because work has disappeared from your life, I want to be clear about one thing from the outset: you are not alone in this experience.

Many capable, thoughtful people go through it more than once. It does not mean you have failed. It does not mean you have fallen behind. It means you are in a transition that deserves care rather than judgement.

You don't need to read this book quickly. You don't need to agree with everything in it. You don't need to turn it into a task. It is meant to be read at your pace, taken in small pieces, or simply held alongside you for a while.

If it helps you feel steadier, more grounded, or less inclined to criticise yourself during this phase, it has done what it was intended to do. Everything else can wait.

CONTENTS

INTRODUCTION

WHO THIS BOOK IS FOR

This book is for capable people whose work has ended and left more than a gap in income.

You may have lost a role suddenly. A contract may have ended without renewal. You may have been "let go", quietly sidelined, or displaced by changes that had nothing to do with your ability.

You are not here because you lack discipline, ambition, or skill.

You are here because something you relied on has disappeared, and the ground hasn't settled yet.

What This Book Helps With

This book helps you:
- steady yourself after work disappears
- reduce panic, shame, and self-blame
- rebuild a sense of structure without forcing productivity
- restore confidence without pretending everything is fine
- take small, meaningful steps back into agency

It is designed for moments of disruption, not peak performance.

What This Book Does Not Promise

This book does not promise:
- fast re-employment
- a perfect plan
- clarity on your entire future
- confidence overnight

It does not offer hacks, hustle, or motivational pressure. What it offers instead is orientation, language, and a way to move forward without rushing yourself.

A Note Before You Begin

Losing work is rarely just a practical problem.

It affects how time feels. How you see yourself. How safe the future appears. How much energy you have available for decisions.

Most advice ignores this. It jumps straight to optimisation: update your CV, apply harder, stay positive, keep learning. For many people, that only increases anxiety and self-doubt.

This book takes a different approach. It assumes that when work disappears, the first task is not strategy, but stabilisation. Not reinvention, but re-orientation. Not confidence, but enough steadiness to take the next small step.

You do not need to fix everything to begin.

How To Read This Book

You do not need to read this book quickly. You do not need to complete every exercise. You do not need to agree with everything in it.

Each chapter has a purpose, and the sequence matters, but your pace does not. Some chapters may feel immediately relevant. Others may not. You are free to skip, pause, or return later. Nothing here is a test.

The practices in this book are optional. They are designed to be small, low-risk, and doable even when energy and confidence are limited. They are experiments, not commitments.

If at any point you feel steadier than when you began, the book is doing its job.

ONE LAST THING

Being without work can make people feel invisible, diminished, or quietly ashamed.

This book starts from a different assumption:

- that you are still a capable adult
- that your response to disruption is understandable
- and that this phase, however uncomfortable, is not the end of your story

You are not broken. You are between chapters.

When you are ready, we'll begin.

Chapter 1

YOU'RE NOT BROKEN

NAMING THE MOMENT

When work disappears, it rarely arrives with a dramatic collapse. There is no single moment that explains everything. Instead, there is a quiet shift.

The days suddenly feel different. Time stretches in unfamiliar ways. Mornings lose their usual shape. Evenings arrive too early or too late. You may find yourself checking the clock more often, or not at all.

Your mind keeps returning to the same questions:
- What now?
- How long will this last?
- What does this say about me?

Not in a neat, logical sequence, but in loops. The same thoughts, revisited at odd moments. In the shower. On a walk. Late at night when the house is quiet.

Outwardly, nothing may look broken. You are still capable. Still competent. Still the same person others know. And yet something essential has shifted. The structure that once held your days together has gone, and without it, even small decisions can feel strangely heavy.

This can be confusing, especially if you are someone who has always coped well. Someone who is used to adapting, solving problems, staying composed. When work disappears, that competence does not vanish, but it no longer has anywhere obvious to land.

So, the experience becomes oddly private. Friends may ask how things are going, and you may find yourself offering short, reassuring answers. "Fine, really." "Just figuring things out." Not because you are hiding anything, but because the truth is difficult to explain. It doesn't feel dramatic enough to justify alarm, yet it carries a constant low-level tension.

You might notice a background hum of unease. Not panic, exactly, but a sense of being slightly unmoored. As if the ground beneath you is still there, but you are no longer certain where to place your weight.

For many people, this is the hardest part. Not the practical problems, but the uncertainty. The loss of rhythm. The absence of something that quietly told you who you were each day when you woke up.

If this is familiar, there is nothing wrong with you. This is what it feels like when a chapter ends before the next one has begun. And for now, naming that is enough.

WHY THIS FEELS SO PERSONAL (AND ISN'T)

When work disappears, it often feels as though something has been taken from you, not just from your life.

Even when you know, logically, that redundancies happen, contracts end, markets shift, and organisations change direction, the loss can land as something more intimate. As though a judgement has been passed. As though a quiet verdict has been delivered on your worth, your relevance, or your place in the world.

This reaction is deeply human.

Work is rarely just a source of income. Over time, it becomes a container for many things we barely notice while they are present. Structure. Routine. A reason to get up at a particular time. A set of problems that belong to you. A sense of contribution that does not need to be explained.

When that container disappears, it can leave more than an empty calendar behind. It removes a framework that once absorbed energy, attention, and identity. Without it, even capable people can feel strangely exposed, as though something that once held them steady has quietly fallen away. This is why the loss can feel so personal, even when it is not.

Modern work encourages us to weave our roles into our sense of self. We introduce ourselves by what we do. We measure progress in titles, projects, and trajectories. Over time, it becomes difficult to separate who we are from the work that has shaped our days.

So, when that work ends, the disruption reaches deeper than most people expect. It is not simply the absence of tasks, but the absence of a mirror. The thing that once reflected competence and usefulness back to you each day is suddenly gone.

Shame often enters at this point, quietly and without invitation. Not the loud kind that demands attention, but the subtler kind that whispers questions in the background:

- Did I miss something?
- Should I have seen this coming?
- What does this say about me?

These questions are rarely fair, and almost never answerable, yet they carry weight all the same.

It is important to be clear about something here. The fact that this feels personal does not mean it is personal. You are responding to the loss of structure, identity, and certainty, not to a hidden truth about yourself. The discomfort is a signal of disruption, not of deficiency. It is the mind and nervous system adjusting to a sudden change in how safety and meaning were organised.

In a culture that prizes independence and self-reliance, this can be hard to accept. Many capable people believe they should be able to absorb change without wobbling. That needing time is a weakness. That steady people stay steady no matter what.

But this expectation is unrealistic. When a significant part of your life disappears, some disorientation is not only normal, it is unavoidable. The mistake is not in feeling unsettled, but in assuming that the feeling must mean something is wrong with you.

Nothing has been revealed. Nothing has been exposed. Something has simply ended, and your system is recalibrating.

Understanding this does not make the situation easy. But it can remove an unnecessary layer of self-blame. And that, in itself, creates a little more room to breathe.

THE LIE OF IMMEDIATE RECOVERY

One of the first pressures to arrive after work disappears is the pressure to recover quickly.

It may not be spoken aloud, but it is often felt. In casual conversations. In well-meaning advice. In the silent comparison with others who appear to have "bounced back" without hesitation.

The message is subtle but persistent: you should be over this by now. You should be applying, planning, reframing, staying positive. You should be proving, to yourself and to others, that this interruption has not touched you too deeply. This expectation is both unrealistic and unhelpful.

Modern culture has developed a strong preference for speed. We admire resilience when it looks like momentum. We praise adaptability when it shows up as immediate action. Pauses, hesitations, and periods of uncertainty are often treated as weaknesses to be overcome rather than signals to be understood.

When work disappears, this bias towards speed can become particularly damaging.

People are often encouraged to move straight into problem-solving mode. Update your CV. Reach out to contacts. Take a course. Reframe the setback as an opportunity. While none of these actions are inherently wrong, taken too early they can add strain rather than relieve it.

Action, when driven by fear rather than steadiness, tends to narrow rather than expand options. It can reinforce the sense that you are behind, that time is being wasted, that you are failing to perform recovery "correctly".

For many people, this creates a second disruption layered on top of the first. Instead of regaining confidence, they find it eroding further. Instead of feeling proactive, they feel exposed. Each application, each unanswered message, each comparison with others becomes another piece of evidence in an internal case against themselves.

This is not resilience. It is self-surveillance. The idea that strength is proven by speed leaves little room for reality. It ignores the fact that sudden change takes time to register. That meaning does not reorganise itself instantly. That energy, once depleted, does not return on command.

Recovery is not a performance. It is a process. There is a difference between moving forward and forcing movement. The first builds agency. The second often deepens exhaustion. Knowing which is which requires patience, not pressure.

This book does not ask you to demonstrate positivity, optimism, or readiness. It does not measure progress by how quickly you appear composed. It assumes that taking time to stabilise is not a delay, but a necessary phase.

You are not failing because you have not "snapped back". You are responding to disruption with honesty. There will be a time for action. There will be a time for direction. But proving resilience is not the task of this moment. For now, it is enough to stop demanding immediate recovery from yourself.

This Is a Transition State, Not a Failure

It is tempting to interpret disruption as a verdict.

When something ends unexpectedly, especially something that once gave structure and meaning, the mind looks for explanations. It wants causes, lessons, conclusions. In the absence of clear answers, it often turns inward: if this has happened, something must have gone wrong.

But there is another way to understand what you are experiencing. What you are in is not a failure state. It is a transition state.

Transitions are uncomfortable precisely because they lack definition. They sit between what was and what will be. The old structures no longer apply, but the new ones have not yet formed. There is movement happening beneath the surface, but it is not visible or directional enough to feel reassuring.

This does not mean nothing is happening. It means the work being done is not yet outward.

Modern careers create more of these moments than previous generations experienced. Roles disappear. Skills are replaced. Organisations restructure. Entire paths that once seemed stable dissolve without warning. The expectation that a working life will unfold smoothly and logically is increasingly out of step with reality.

Yet many of the stories we tell about success have not caught up. They still imply continuity. They still reward linear narratives. They still treat disruption as an anomaly rather than a feature. When your experience does not match those stories, it is easy to assume you are the problem. You are not.

Being between chapters is not a personal deficiency. It is a phase that has patterns, even if it does not yet have clarity. It comes with predictable feelings: uncertainty, self-doubt, restlessness, a pull to rush ahead and a simultaneous reluctance to move at all.

Understanding this matters, because it changes what progress looks like.

In a failure frame, the task is to correct mistakes quickly and return to the previous trajectory. In a transition frame, the task is different. It is to stabilise, to regain footing, and to allow a new direction to emerge without forcing it prematurely.

This is why the order matters. Stabilisation comes before strategy. Movement comes before clarity. Agency comes before ambition.

These are not slogans. They are practical responses to uncertainty. They acknowledge that when the old chapter has ended, the next one cannot be written immediately. There is always a space in between.

This book is designed to support you in that space. Not by rushing you through it, but by helping you understand where you are, why it feels the way it does, and how to move forward without losing yourself in the process.

You are not standing still because you have failed. You are paused because something is changing. And that distinction changes everything.

WHAT THIS BOOK IS (AND ISN'T)

Before going any further, it is worth being clear about what this book is here to do, and what it is not.

When work disappears, people are often handed advice that arrives with urgency. Instructions. Frameworks. Optimisation strategies. Lists of things they should be doing by now. Much of it is well intentioned, but it assumes a level of energy, confidence, and clarity that may not yet be available.

This book does not make that assumption.

What this book is:

- It is a steady companion for a period of disruption. It is written for people whose cognitive and emotional bandwidth may be reduced, and who need orientation more than instruction.
- It is practical but not demanding. The ideas and exercises that follow are designed to restore agency without creating pressure. They are meant to be used lightly, adapted, or set aside as needed.
- This book is concerned with momentum, not mastery. With stabilising your footing, not optimising your future. It assumes that progress, at this stage, will be uneven and sometimes invisible.

What this book is not:

- It is not a motivation manual. It will not ask you to "reframe" everything as an opportunity or to summon confidence on command.
- It is not a rebranding exercise. You will not be asked to polish a story or present yourself as more certain than you feel.
- It is not a promise of fast outcomes. There are no guarantees here, only a way of moving forward that respects where you are starting from.

Most importantly, this book is not here to judge you. You are not required to prove resilience, positivity, or readiness. You do not need to have answers before you begin. You do not need to act on every idea for this book to be useful.

If at any point you find yourself feeling steadier, clearer, or more capable of taking the next small step, that is enough.

This book does not measure success by how quickly you return to work, or by how convincing your plans sound. It measures success by the quiet restoration of agency, confidence, and self-trust.

Everything else comes later.

PERMISSION TO PAUSE

Before moving on, it is worth pausing here. Not to decide anything. Not to plan what comes next. Simply to notice where you are.

When work disappears, there is often a sense that time has become dangerous. That every unstructured day is a risk. That stillness must be justified or explained. This can create an internal pressure to keep moving, even when movement feels forced or draining.

This book does not ask that of you.

Pausing is not the same as giving up. It is not avoidance, and it is not indulgence. In moments of transition, pausing is often how the system settles enough to respond rather than react.

Nothing in your life needs to be fixed today. You do not need to know what you will do next, how long this phase will last, or what the eventual outcome will be. Those answers come later, and they arrive more reliably once steadiness has returned.

For now, stabilisation is progress. If all this chapter has done is help you feel a little less alone, a little less personally at fault, and a little more grounded than when you began, then it has done its job.

You are still the same capable person you were before work disappeared. Your skills have not evaporated. Your experience has not been erased. What has changed is the context around you, not the substance of who you are.

There will be time for understanding. There will be time for action. There will be time for direction.

This chapter is simply about creating enough calm to continue.

When you are ready, the next chapter will help make sense of what is happening beneath the surface, and why this phase feels as challenging as it does.

For now, you are allowed to stop here.

Chapter 2

WHAT'S ACTUALLY GOING ON HERE

THE WORLD OF WORK CHANGED FASTER THAN WE DID

For much of the last century, work followed a set of assumptions that felt solid, even if they were never perfect.

Roles tended to endure. Skills accumulated steadily. Progress was expected to be gradual and, if not predictable, at least understandable in hindsight. People planned their lives around the idea that work would change occasionally but rarely vanish without warning. Those assumptions no longer hold.

In many industries, roles now disappear faster than individuals can adapt to them. Organisations restructure frequently, not because people have failed, but because conditions change quickly and unpredictably. Decisions are made to reduce risk, preserve cash, or respond to forces that sit far beyond any one person's influence.

From the inside, these changes often feel abrupt and personal. From the outside, they are structural.

Work has become more fragmented. Contracts shorten. Teams assemble and dissolve. Entire functions are redefined or removed as technology, markets, and priorities shift. In this environment, continuity is no longer the default, even for capable, experienced people.

What makes this particularly disorienting is that many of us were shaped by a different set of expectations. We were taught, implicitly or explicitly, that effort leads to stability. That competence protects you. That if you perform well and keep developing, work will generally be there.

When reality breaks from that story, the gap can feel like failure. But the story itself has not kept pace with the world it is meant to explain.

The result is a quiet mismatch. People experience disruption but lack a framework for understanding it. Without that framework, it is easy to assume that what has happened reflects a personal shortcoming rather than a systemic shift.

This is why so many capable people are caught off guard when work disappears. Not because they were careless or unprepared, but because the ground moved in ways they were never trained to expect.

None of this makes the situation easier. It does, however, make it clearer. Losing work in the modern world is no longer an outlier event. It is a common feature of careers shaped by rapid change. The problem is not that people are failing more often, but that the conditions around them are less stable than they once were.

Understanding this does not remove the disruption. But it can remove a layer of unnecessary self-blame. You are not uniquely behind. You are not alone in this experience. And you are not imagining how sudden it feels.

The world of work has changed, and many people are navigating the consequences without a map.

Why Your Brain Is Struggling With This

When work disappears, many people are surprised by how much harder thinking becomes.

Simple decisions feel heavier than they should. Concentration fades quickly. Confidence drops, even though ability has not changed. You may find yourself overthinking small choices while avoiding larger ones altogether.

This is not a failure of discipline or motivation. The human brain is designed to cope best when the world is reasonably predictable. Routine, rhythm, and expectation create a sense of safety that allows attention to be directed outward, towards problem-solving, learning, and contribution.

When a major source of predictability disappears, the brain shifts priorities. Instead of optimising for performance, it begins scanning for risk. Instead of focusing on long-term plans, it becomes preoccupied with short-term uncertainty. Energy is diverted towards monitoring and control, even when there is nothing obvious to control.

This shift is subtle, but it is costly.

Mental bandwidth narrows. Tasks that once felt manageable require more effort. Decisions that would normally be automatic start to demand conscious thought. The result is often a sense of fog, fatigue, or restlessness that is difficult to explain to others.

This is why people often feel "less like themselves" after work ends. It is not that capability has vanished. It is that the system is under load. Uncertainty consumes attention, leaving less available for creativity, planning, or confident action.

Confidence tends to be one of the first things to dip, not because it was fragile to begin with, but because it relies on feedback loops that have been interrupted. When work is present, competence is reinforced daily through tasks completed, problems solved, and contributions made.

When those signals disappear, the mind fills the gap with questions:
- Am I still useful?
- Am I falling behind?
- Am I doing this right?

These questions are not signs of insecurity. They are signs of missing information.

In this state, effort can easily be misdirected. People try to think their way back to certainty, pushing for answers before the conditions for clarity have returned. This often increases frustration rather than resolving it.

Understanding what is happening here matters, because it changes how you respond. If the brain is struggling because it is adjusting to uncertainty, the solution is not to demand more output from it. It is to reduce unnecessary strain, restore a sense of safety where possible, and allow capacity to return gradually.

Nothing has gone wrong inside you. Your system is doing exactly what it is designed to do when predictability disappears. It is protecting you, even if the experience feels uncomfortable.

Recognising this can make the difference between fighting yourself and working with what is actually happening.

THE HIDDEN COST OF UNCERTAINTY

Uncertainty is often treated as a minor inconvenience, something to be endured while a better answer is found.

In reality, it is one of the most exhausting states a person can be in. Bad news, while painful, has edges. It creates a situation that can be reacted to, planned around, or accepted. Uncertainty does not. It keeps the mind suspended, scanning for information that never quite arrives.

When work disappears, uncertainty expands in several directions at once. There is uncertainty about time: how long will this last? Uncertainty about money: what happens if it takes longer than expected? Uncertainty about identity: what does this mean for who I am now?

Each unanswered question draws a small but persistent amount of energy. On their own, they may seem manageable. Together, they create a constant background drain.

This is why people often feel tired without having done very much.

Energy is being spent not on visible action, but on holding open multiple possibilities at once. The mind keeps returning to the same unknowns, trying to resolve them, even when there is no new information available.

Planning becomes difficult in this state. Plans rely on assumptions. They require a sense of what is likely enough to commit to. When the future feels unstable, every assumption feels fragile. Even sensible plans can feel premature, or strangely hollow, because they rest on foundations that do not yet feel secure.

Time can also begin to feel distorted. Days may blur together or feel uncomfortably empty. At the same time, there may be a sense that time is running out, even when there is no immediate deadline. This combination of spaciousness and pressure is deeply unsettling.

None of this is a sign that you are handling the situation badly. It is a natural response to extended uncertainty.

What often makes this worse is the way uncertainty is interpreted. In cultures that value decisiveness and confidence, not knowing is frequently equated with weakness. Waiting is seen as passivity. Hesitation is treated as avoidance.

But uncertainty is not a character flaw. It is a condition.

Until some of it resolves, either through time, information, or stabilisation, the system remains under strain. Pushing for certainty too early does not relieve that strain. It usually increases it.

Recognising the cost of uncertainty allows for a different response. Instead of asking yourself why you are not doing more, you can begin to notice where energy is being quietly consumed. Instead of demanding clarity, you can focus on reducing unnecessary sources of tension and restoring a sense of steadiness where possible.

This does not make uncertainty disappear. But it can stop it from dominating everything else and that creates space for the next step: understanding why so much well-meaning advice fails precisely at this point.

Why Common Advice Fails in This Phase

Much of the advice people receive when work disappears is well intentioned.

Friends want to be helpful. Colleagues want to reassure. Articles and posts aim to motivate. The problem is not a lack of goodwill. It is that most advice is designed for a different state of mind than the one you are in now.

Common guidance assumes a level of stability that may no longer be present.

Advice to "update your CV", "start networking", or "stay positive" presumes that you have enough clarity, energy, and confidence to translate those instructions into meaningful action. When you don't, the advice can feel strangely hollow, or even quietly accusatory.

It can leave you thinking that the real problem is not the situation, but your response to it.

CV-first advice is a good example. CVs are tools for compressing the past into a clean, linear story. They work best when there is continuity, confidence, and a clear sense of direction. During disruption, those conditions rarely exist. Being asked to present yourself as coherent and certain when you are still stabilising can amplify self-doubt rather than reduce it.

Networking advice often fails for similar reasons. Reaching out requires a sense of what you are asking for and what you are offering. When identity and direction feel provisional, those conversations can feel exposed and uncomfortable. The result is often avoidance, followed by guilt for avoiding something you have been told is essential.

Forced optimism can be the most unhelpful of all. Encouragement to "stay positive" usually aims to lift morale, but it can inadvertently dismiss the reality of what is being experienced. When reassurance skips over fear and uncertainty, it can make those feelings harder to admit, even to yourself.

None of this means the advice is wrong in principle. It means it is mistimed.

There is a difference between guidance that helps once steadiness has returned and guidance that lands too early. When the timing is off, even sensible suggestions can increase pressure rather than provide support.

This is why so many capable people find themselves oscillating between bursts of forced activity and periods of withdrawal. They are trying to follow instructions that do not match their current capacity.

Understanding this matters because it shifts the question. Instead of asking, "Why can't I follow this advice?" The more useful question becomes, "Is this the right advice for this phase?" Often, it is not.

This book does not reject action, visibility, or planning. It simply recognises that those things work best when they are built on steadiness rather than urgency.

The task of this phase is not to perform recovery convincingly, but to rebuild the conditions that make genuine progress possible.

What This Phase Actually Requires

If much of the difficulty of this moment comes from uncertainty, reduced capacity, and mistimed expectations, then the response needs to match those conditions.

This phase does not require intensity. It does not require constant effort. And it does not require you to have answers. What it requires, first and foremost, is stabilisation.

Stabilisation is not inactivity. It is the deliberate creation of enough steadiness to allow the system to settle. It means reducing unnecessary inputs, protecting limited energy, and restoring small, reliable points of control in daily life.

In practical terms, this often looks quieter than people expect. It may involve narrowing focus rather than expanding it. Letting go of tasks that are draining without being useful. Creating gentle structure where days have become shapeless. Choosing actions that restore a sense of agency, even if they do not immediately move you closer to an outcome.

This can feel counterintuitive in a culture that equates progress with visible motion. But when capacity is reduced, the goal is not to do more, but to do what supports recovery of energy and confidence.

Clarity rarely appears under pressure. It emerges once the background noise has lowered. This is why stabilisation comes before strategy, and movement comes before direction. Small, low-stakes actions can rebuild trust in your ability to act without demanding certainty about where those actions will ultimately lead.

At this stage, the most important shifts are internal. Feeling a little calmer than you did before. Finding that decisions take less effort. Noticing moments where curiosity replaces dread.

These are not signs that nothing is happening. They are signals that the system is beginning to recover.

This book is structured around that reality. The chapters that follow will look more closely at the patterns that keep people stuck, introduce a simple way of orienting yourself during uncertainty, and offer practices designed to rebuild momentum without pressure.

For now, it is enough to understand this, you are not struggling because you are doing this wrong, you are struggling because this phase has specific demands, and they are rarely acknowledged.

Once those demands are recognised, the path forward becomes quieter, but clearer.

Chapter 3

THE TRAP MOST PEOPLE FALL INTO

WHY WE REACH FOR TRAPS AT ALL

When work disappears, people rarely respond by doing nothing. Most respond by trying to regain control.

They plan. They research. They prepare. They tell themselves they are being sensible, responsible, proactive. From the outside, these behaviours often look like exactly what should be happening. From the inside, they usually feel necessary.

This is why the patterns explored in this chapter are best understood not as mistakes, but as coping strategies. They are the mind's attempt to reduce uncertainty, restore safety, and protect a sense of competence during a period of disruption.

When familiar structures vanish, the system looks for substitutes.

Planning creates the feeling of direction. Learning creates the feeling of progress. Waiting for confidence creates the feeling of self-respect. Comparison creates the feeling of orientation, even when it hurts.

Each of these responses offers short-term relief. They provide something to hold onto when the ground feels unstable. They reassure us that we are not ignoring the situation, that we are being diligent, that we are taking it seriously.

The problem is not that these responses are irrational. The problem is that they work just well enough to keep us repeating them, without resolving the uncertainty they are meant to address.

Over time, what began as a sensible response can become a holding pattern.

People do not get stuck because they are lazy or avoidant. They get stuck because the strategies they are using reduce discomfort without restoring agency. They soothe anxiety in the moment but leave the deeper questions untouched.

This is why these patterns are best described as traps. Not because they are foolish, but because they are self-reinforcing. Each one makes sense in isolation. Together, they can quietly prolong the very state they are meant to escape.

Recognising a trap does not require self-criticism. It requires honesty.

Most capable people fall into at least one of these patterns during periods of transition. Many cycle between several, depending on energy, mood, or external pressure. None of this says anything negative about who you are. It simply reflects how humans respond when certainty disappears.

The sections that follow are not here to diagnose you. They are here to help you notice where effort may be misdirected, and where small interruptions could make a meaningful difference.

Nothing in this chapter requires you to stop trying. It simply invites you to try differently.

Trap One: Over-Planning as Control

Planning is one of the most socially approved responses to uncertainty.

When work disappears, the instinct to plan can feel not only sensible, but responsible. Plans promise order. They offer a way to impose structure on a situation that feels chaotic. They suggest that if you think hard enough, map carefully enough, or anticipate every possibility, clarity will eventually emerge.

For many capable people, planning is a familiar strength. It is how problems have been solved in the past. When faced with disruption, it is natural to reach for the tools that have worked before.

This is what makes over-planning such a convincing trap.

The shift from useful planning to over-planning is often subtle. It does not announce itself as avoidance. It presents as diligence. Time is spent refining options, exploring scenarios, researching paths, and constructing frameworks for what might come next.

On the surface, it looks like progress. Underneath, something else is happening.

Planning feels safer than action because it carries no immediate risk. There is no exposure. No chance of rejection. No feedback that might challenge the story you are telling yourself. As long as you are planning, you remain protected from the uncertainty that comes with testing an idea in the real world.

The problem is that planning is meant to support movement, not replace it.

When clarity is treated as a prerequisite for action, planning becomes endless by design. There is always another scenario to consider, another variable to account for, another version of the plan that might finally feel solid enough.

Meanwhile, confidence does not return. Agency does not increase. The sense of being in motion remains just out of reach.

Over time, planning can begin to reinforce the very uncertainty it is meant to resolve. Each revision suggests that the previous one was insufficient. Each new framework implies that the answer lies just one more layer of thinking away.

What started as a way to regain control quietly becomes a way to postpone engagement.

This trap is particularly effective because it is rarely challenged by others. Planning looks like effort. It sounds like responsibility. It allows you to tell yourself, and anyone who asks, that you are "working on it". But effort is not the same as movement.

Recognising over-planning does not mean abandoning thought or preparation. It means noticing when planning has stopped serving action and has started serving safety instead.

This is not a failure of discipline or courage. It is a sign that certainty is being demanded before it can reasonably exist.

Later in this book, you will be invited to experiment with a different sequence, one where small movement is allowed to create clarity, rather than waiting for clarity to permit movement.

For now, it is enough to notice whether planning has become a place to hide.

Trap Two: Endless Learning Without Application

Learning is rarely questioned as a response to disruption.

When work disappears, many people are encouraged to "upskill", "reskill", or "invest in themselves". Courses are recommended. Books are bought. Podcasts are queued. On the surface, this seems like the most constructive thing a person could do. And often, it is.

Learning becomes a trap only when it replaces application rather than supporting it.

For capable people, learning offers a particularly comfortable refuge. It restores a sense of progress without requiring exposure. It allows you to feel productive, improving, and responsible, while remaining safely out of view. You are not failing; you are preparing.

This makes learning an especially persuasive response during periods of uncertainty. The shift into the trap is rarely deliberate. It begins with genuine curiosity or sensible preparation. Over time, however, learning can become a holding pattern. One course leads to another. One book sparks a list of related titles. Each new insight promises that once it is fully understood, confidence will return.

The problem is not a lack of information. Most people in this position already know far more than they are currently using. The gap is not knowledge, but trust. Trust that what you already have is enough to act with, even imperfectly.

Endless learning delays that moment of trust. By staying in learning mode, identity remains provisional. You are still becoming. Still not quite ready. Still one step away from contribution. This can feel responsible, but it quietly reinforces the idea that you are not yet legitimate.

Over time, this can erode confidence rather than build it. You become well-informed but hesitant. Insightful but unpractised. Prepared but unseen.

Learning without application also carries a hidden cost. It keeps the centre of gravity inward. Attention is focused on consumption rather than contribution. Feedback remains theoretical rather than real. Without testing ideas in the world, there is nothing to correct, refine, or build on.

This is why confidence rarely returns through learning alone.

Confidence is rebuilt through use. Through doing something small and seeing that you can. Through applying knowledge imperfectly and surviving the outcome. Through discovering that competence is not erased by uncertainty.

None of this means you should stop learning. It means learning needs somewhere to land.

Later in this book, the practices you are offered will favour application over accumulation. Small experiments. Low-risk actions. Opportunities to use what you already know, rather than waiting to know more.

For now, it is enough to ask a simple question: is learning helping me move, or helping me wait?

TRAP THREE: WAITING FOR CONFIDENCE TO RETURN

One of the most common reasons people delay action during periods of disruption is the belief that confidence must return first.

They tell themselves they will move once they feel like themselves again. Once the fog lifts. Once the anxiety settles. Once they feel more certain, more grounded, more ready.

This belief feels reasonable. Confidence is often treated as a prerequisite for action, a sign that the timing is right. Without it, acting can feel reckless or premature.

The problem is that confidence rarely works this way. Confidence is not a resource that quietly regenerates on its own while you wait. It is a response to evidence. It grows when you see yourself act and survive the outcome. It strengthens through use, not through reflection alone.

When work disappears, the feedback loops that once reinforced confidence are interrupted. Tasks are no longer completed. Contributions are no longer recognised. Small daily signals of competence quietly vanish.

In this environment, waiting for confidence to return is like waiting for a muscle to strengthen without moving it.

The longer action is postponed, the more distant confidence can feel. Hesitation is interpreted as further proof that you are not ready. Each delay subtly reinforces the belief that something is missing.

This creates a self-sustaining pattern. You wait because confidence is low. Confidence remains low because you are waiting.

From the inside, this can feel like caution. From the outside, it often looks like avoidance. In truth, it is neither. It is a reasonable response to uncertainty combined with a mistaken assumption about how confidence works.

Confidence does not require certainty. It does not require a clear plan or a fully formed identity. It requires small experiences of agency, even in imperfect conditions.

This does not mean forcing yourself into high-stakes situations before you are ready. It means recognising that confidence is rebuilt through low-risk movement, not through internal readiness checks.

Later in this book, the practices you are offered are designed with this in mind. They prioritise actions that are small enough to feel safe, yet real enough to restore trust in your ability to act.

For now, it is enough to notice this pattern.

If you have been waiting to feel confident before moving, it may not be a lack of courage that is holding you back. It may simply be the absence of movement.

Confidence has not disappeared. It has been paused. And like most things that are paused, it resumes once you press play.

TRAP FOUR: COMPARING TRAJECTORIES

When work disappears, comparison has a way of creeping in quietly.

You may not seek it out deliberately. It often arrives through casual scrolling, brief updates, or passing mentions of other people's progress. Someone announces a new role. Someone shares a promotion. Someone appears to be moving forward with certainty and momentum.

In moments of transition, these signals can feel amplified. What might once have registered as neutral information now carries weight. Other people's movement is interpreted not just as their success, but as evidence of your own stagnation. Their clarity becomes a mirror in which your uncertainty looks like failure.

This is not because comparison is new, but because context has changed. When you are grounded in work, comparison is filtered through daily experience. You know what you are contributing. You have a sense of your own trajectory, even if it is imperfect. When that anchor disappears, comparison fills the gap. It offers a false sense of orientation.

Looking at others can feel like a way of working out where you should be, how fast you should be moving, or what you should be aiming for next. In reality, it collapses complexity into a single, misleading dimension.

You see outcomes without seeing process. You see announcements without seeing uncertainty. You see direction without seeing the detours that preceded it.

Most importantly, you see someone else's chapter and judge it against your own, without accounting for the fact that you are in different places in the story.

This is what makes comparison so corrosive during transition. It strips away context and replaces it with a crude hierarchy. Ahead or behind. Winning or losing. Progressing or stuck. Once this frame takes hold, it becomes difficult to recognise your own movement, especially when that movement is internal or preparatory.

Comparison also tends to target the most visible people, not the most representative ones. You are unlikely to compare yourself to those who are also uncertain, paused, or quietly rebuilding. Their stories are less visible, and therefore easier to ignore.

The result is a distorted sense of reality.

You begin to believe that everyone else has found their footing while you alone are struggling to regain yours. This belief is not supported by evidence, but it can feel convincing all the same.

The trap here is not noticing others' progress. It is using it as a measure of your own worth or timing. Careers do not unfold at a uniform pace. They move in bursts, stalls, pivots, and restarts. Periods of visibility often follow long stretches of uncertainty that never make it into public view.

Comparing trajectories without context does not motivate. It paralyses.

Recognising this pattern is not about withdrawing from the world or avoiding information altogether. It is about noticing when comparison has stopped being informative and has started becoming self-punishing.

If you find yourself feeling smaller, more anxious, or more rushed after looking outward, that is not a call to try harder. It is a signal that the frame you are using is unhelpful.

You are not behind. You are between chapters. And that makes comparison a poor guide for what comes next.

How These Traps Keep You Stuck (Without You Realising)

Individually, the traps described in this chapter can seem harmless.

Planning feels responsible. Learning feels productive. Waiting for confidence feels sensible. Comparing trajectories feels informative.

Each one offers a way to manage discomfort without doing anything obviously wrong. This is why they are so easy to fall into, and so hard to recognise as limiting. The problem emerges when these responses begin to interact.

Planning postpones action until clarity arrives. Learning postpones action until readiness is achieved. Waiting for confidence postpones action until feelings improve. Comparison amplifies the sense that action must be perfect to count.

Together, they create a closed loop. Action is delayed because conditions do not feel right. Conditions do not improve because action is delayed. Over time, this loop is experienced not as a choice, but as being stuck.

From the inside, it often feels like effort without traction.

You are thinking, preparing, monitoring, and evaluating, yet nothing seems to move forward. This can be deeply frustrating, especially for people who are used to making progress through diligence and competence.

What is often missed is that these traps reduce uncertainty in the short term without increasing agency in the long term.

They soothe anxiety, but they do not restore momentum. They create the feeling of being busy or responsible, but not the experience of moving.

This is why "stuckness" is rarely about a lack of motivation. It is more often the result of self-protection running quietly in the background. The system is trying to avoid risk, rejection, and further destabilisation by insisting on better conditions before acting.

There is nothing wrong with that instinct. It exists to keep you safe. The difficulty arises when safety becomes the only criterion for movement. In that case, action is always deferred, because uncertainty never fully disappears on its own.

Understanding this changes how you respond. Instead of asking why you are not doing more, you can begin to see where effort is being absorbed by patterns that do not lead anywhere. Instead of trying to push harder, you can look for ways to interrupt the loop gently, without overwhelming yourself.

Being stuck, in this sense, is not a character defect. It is a predictable outcome of understandable strategies applied for too long.

Once this is recognised, the problem becomes easier to work with. You do not need to eliminate these traps entirely. You do not need to force yourself into bravery or decisiveness. You simply need a different orientation, one that allows movement to rebuild confidence rather than waiting for confidence to permit movement.

A Gentle Interruption

Once a pattern has been recognised, the question is no longer how to escape it completely. It is how to interrupt it.

The traps described in this chapter are not enemies to be defeated. They are habits that formed in response to uncertainty. Trying to eliminate them all at once would simply replace one form of pressure with another.

A more useful approach is quieter. Interruption does not mean stopping everything. It means noticing when a familiar response has taken over and choosing, just once, to respond slightly differently.

Instead of planning again, you might take one small step without a full map. Instead of learning more, you might use something you already know. Instead of waiting to feel confident, you might act in a way that builds confidence. Instead of comparing, you might return attention to what is within reach today.

These are not dramatic shifts. They are small changes in sequence.

Not more effort, but better orientation. Not elimination, but redirection. Not force, but permission.

This is why the next chapter does not offer a system to follow or a plan to execute. It introduces a simple way of orienting yourself during uncertainty, one that prioritises agency over ambition and movement over certainty.

The aim is not to fix you. It is to help you move without losing yourself in the process. You do not need to be ready for everything that comes next. You only need to be willing to interrupt the loop, gently and briefly, enough to let something new begin.

The next chapter explores how to do that.

Chapter 4

A BETTER WAY THROUGH THIS TRANSITION

WHY YOU DON'T NEED A PLAN RIGHT NOW

When work disappears, the instinct to plan often returns with force.

Plans promise certainty. They offer a sense of direction when the future feels undefined. They suggest that if you can just think far enough ahead, the anxiety will ease and momentum will return.

In stable conditions, this instinct is often helpful. Plans work when the terrain is familiar and the variables are reasonably predictable. They allow effort to be organised and progress to be measured. But during transition, those conditions rarely apply.

When the old chapter has ended and the next one has not yet begun, the ground is still shifting. Information is incomplete. Energy is uneven. Identity itself may feel provisional. In this state, planning can quickly become a source of strain rather than support.

The problem is not planning itself. It is the timing. Plans assume answers to questions that do not yet have answers. They require you to commit to a version of the future before you have regained enough stability to trust that commitment. When those assumptions inevitably wobble, the plan collapses, and with it, confidence.

This is why planning often leads to repeated revisions during periods of disruption. Each new plan feels necessary, but none feel quite right. The result is not clarity, but fatigue.

It can feel as though you are failing at planning, when in fact planning is failing you.

There is a quieter alternative. Instead of trying to decide where you are going, you can focus on how you are moving. Instead of forcing direction, you can develop orientation. Orientation does not require certainty. It asks only for a sense of what supports you and what does not, right now.

This shift matters.

Direction is fragile when conditions are unstable. Orientation is not. It allows you to take steps without knowing exactly where they will lead, and to adjust as new information emerges.

You do not need a five-year plan, a clear narrative, or a polished strategy to move forward from here. You need a way to make decisions that does not depend on having everything figured out.

This chapter introduces that way. Not as a map to follow, but as a compass to carry.

FROM MAPS TO COMPASSES

Most advice about careers is built around maps. Maps show routes. They outline steps. They assume you know where you are starting from and where you are trying to go. In stable terrain, maps are useful. They allow you to move efficiently and measure progress along the way. But maps depend on the ground staying the same.

When the landscape shifts, maps lose their usefulness quickly. Paths disappear. Landmarks move. Routes that once made sense lead nowhere. Trying to follow an outdated map in unfamiliar terrain does not create progress, it creates frustration.

Periods of transition are exactly this kind of terrain. When work disappears, you are no longer navigating a known route. You are moving through uncertainty, where old reference points no longer apply and new ones have not yet emerged. In these conditions, asking for a map is asking for something that cannot reliably exist.

What helps instead is a compass. A compass does not tell you where to go. It does not lay out a sequence of steps. It gives you a bearing. It helps you stay oriented when you cannot see far ahead.

Compasses work precisely because they do not rely on detailed knowledge of the terrain. They remain useful when conditions change, when visibility is poor, and when the path forward is not yet clear.

This is the kind of guidance that works during transition.

Rather than trying to plan your way out of uncertainty, you can carry a small set of principles that help you decide, in the moment, whether a particular action is likely to support or undermine your recovery of confidence and agency.

The aim is not to optimise every move. It is to avoid getting lost. Maps encourage certainty before movement. Compasses allow movement without certainty. This distinction matters.

When you are between chapters, insisting on a map often keeps you stuck. Carrying a compass allows you to take steps, learn from them, and adjust your direction as you go.

The framework introduced in this chapter is deliberately compass-like. It is light, flexible, and repeatable. It does not tell you what to do next. It helps you evaluate whether what you are doing makes sense for this phase of your journey.

You do not need to abandon planning forever. There will be a time when maps are useful again. But for now, while the terrain is unfamiliar, a compass will serve you better.

THE BETWEEN CHAPTERS COMPASS

The Between Chapters Compass is not a plan. It does not tell you what role to pursue, what decision to make, or how long this phase should last. It exists for a simpler purpose: to help you orient yourself while clarity is still forming.

When work disappears, many people try to solve the wrong problem. They look for certainty when what they actually need is steadiness. They look for direction when what they need first is agency.

The compass addresses that gap. Rather than asking, "What should I do next?" It asks, "Does this support or undermine my ability to move through this phase with dignity?"

This is a subtle shift, but a powerful one.

The compass is made up of a small set of principles that can be carried lightly and returned to often. They are not rules. They are not steps. They are lenses you can use to evaluate choices when the future is still unclear.

Each principle reflects a simple truth about transition:
- that stability comes before strategy
- that movement creates clarity
- that agency matters more than ambition
- that energy is a more reliable guide than optimisation

Together, these principles help you decide how to move, even when you do not yet know where you are going.

Importantly, the compass is not something you apply perfectly. You will forget it. You will override it. You will sometimes act against it. That does not make it ineffective.

A compass is useful precisely because it can be checked quickly and imperfectly. Even a brief glance can prevent you from drifting too far off course.

This framework is designed to do the same. You might use it to sense-check a decision. To notice when pressure is creeping in. To choose between two imperfect options. Or simply to reassure yourself that a small step is enough for now.

The compass does not remove uncertainty. It helps you move without being dominated by it.

In the sections that follow, each principle is explored in turn. Not as theory, but as a way of staying oriented while this transition is ongoing.

You do not need to memorise them. You do not need to apply them all at once. You only need to know they are there.

The first principle begins where this phase always begins: with stability.

PRINCIPLE ONE: STABILITY BEFORE STRATEGY

Stability is often misunderstood. It is frequently confused with stagnation, hesitation, or a lack of ambition. In cultures that prize momentum and visible progress, stabilising can look like doing nothing at all.

During transition, the opposite is true.

Stability is the foundation that makes everything else possible. Without it, strategy becomes fragile and short-lived. Decisions are made from anxiety rather than intention. Effort is spent reacting rather than choosing.

When work disappears, stability is usually the first thing to erode. Days lose their rhythm. Boundaries blur. Energy fluctuates unpredictably. Small stresses begin to accumulate, not because they are large, but because there is no longer a structure to absorb them.

In this state, jumping straight to strategy can feel urgent, but it often backfires. Plans built on unstable ground collapse quickly, reinforcing the sense that you cannot trust yourself to move forward.

This is why the first principle of the Between Chapters Compass is stability before strategy.

Stability does not mean returning to your old routine or recreating work where none exists. It means establishing enough steadiness to think, decide, and act without being overwhelmed.

This kind of stability is usually built quietly. It may involve creating gentle structure around your day, not to maximise productivity, but to restore predictability. It may mean protecting your energy more deliberately, saying no to things that drain you without giving anything back. It may mean narrowing your focus rather than expanding it, reducing the number of decisions you are carrying at once.

None of this is a retreat.

Stability is an active choice to reduce unnecessary strain. It is a way of signalling to yourself that you are safe enough to move, even if you do not yet know in which direction.

Importantly, stability is temporary. It is not the goal of this phase. It is the condition that allows the next phase to emerge. Once steadiness has returned, strategy becomes easier, not harder. Clarity has somewhere to land.

This principle also acts as a guardrail. When you find yourself pushing for answers, forcing plans, or feeling increasingly agitated by the lack of progress, it is often a sign that stability has been overlooked. Returning to it is not going backwards. It is re-establishing the ground from which movement can occur.

You do not need to earn the right to stabilise. You do not need permission to slow down. Stability is not a delay. It is the first step.

Principle Two: Movement Before Clarity

Once stability has begun to return, the next temptation is to wait for clarity.

Clarity feels like permission. It promises confidence, direction, and reassurance that you are about to make the right choice. In uncertain moments, it is natural to believe that once things make sense again, movement will follow.

In practice, clarity rarely arrives this way.

Clarity is not something you discover by thinking harder. It is something that emerges through contact with reality. It is shaped by use, feedback, and experience, not by internal certainty.

This is why movement comes before clarity.

When you take a small step, even without a clear destination, you generate information. You learn what drains you and what gives you energy. You discover what feels aligned and what does not. You regain a sense of agency by acting and observing the result.

Waiting for clarity postpones all of this.

This principle directly interrupts several of the traps explored earlier. Over-planning delays movement until answers are complete. Endless learning delays movement until readiness is achieved. Waiting for confidence delays movement until feelings improve.

Each assumes that understanding must precede action. In reality, it is often the other way round.

Movement does not need to be decisive to be useful. It does not need to be visible, public, or impressive. It only needs to be real.

Small movements are especially powerful during transition. They carry low risk, but they restore trust. They provide evidence that you can act without collapsing, even when conditions are imperfect.

This is not about forcing yourself into action when you are depleted. It builds on the stability that has already been established. Movement that comes too early can overwhelm. Movement that comes too late can prolong uncertainty.

The compass helps you sense the difference.

A useful question at this stage is not, "Is this the right move?" It is, "Is this a move that helps me learn?"

When movement is treated as exploration rather than commitment, clarity becomes a by-product rather than a prerequisite.

You do not need to know where you will end up to begin moving. You only need to be willing to let small steps teach you what thinking alone cannot.

Clarity follows movement, not the other way round.

Principle Three: Agency Before Ambition

When work disappears, ambition often becomes distorted.

Some people cling to it tightly, using future goals as a way to reassure themselves that everything will be fine. Others lose touch with it altogether, finding that what once motivated them now feels distant or irrelevant. Both responses are understandable.

Ambition is usually built on stability. It assumes a degree of control over circumstances and a clear sense of trajectory. During transition, those conditions are disrupted, and ambition can begin to feel either forced or hollow.

This is why agency matters more than ambition at this stage.

Agency is the sense that you still have choice. That you can influence your day, your actions, and your responses, even in small ways. It does not require a grand vision or a long-term plan. It requires only the experience of deciding and acting.

When agency erodes, ambition becomes brittle.

People begin to set goals that feel performative rather than meaningful, or they abandon goal-setting entirely because it no longer feels safe to want things. In both cases, self-trust is undermined.

Restoring agency comes first. Agency can be rebuilt quietly. By choosing how you structure your time. By deciding what you will and will not engage with. By taking small actions that confirm you still have influence, even when outcomes remain uncertain.

These choices may not look ambitious. They may not move you closer to a visible result. But they matter.

Agency is what allows ambition to return in a healthy form later on. Without it, ambition tends to become either overwhelming or absent.

This principle also acts as a safeguard. When you feel pressure to set goals you do not yet believe in, to chase outcomes that feel misaligned, or to present yourself as more certain than you are, it is often a sign that ambition has raced ahead of agency.

Returning to agency is not a step backwards. It is a recalibration.

You do not need to know what you want to achieve next in order to act. You need only to know that the action you are taking is chosen rather than forced.

Ambition can wait. Agency cannot.

Once agency is restored, ambition has something solid to grow from.

PRINCIPLE FOUR: ENERGY BEFORE OPTIMISATION

Optimisation is seductive. When uncertainty sets in, the instinct to improve, refine, and perfect can feel like a way back to control. If you just do things better, more efficiently, or more strategically, the thinking goes, momentum will return.

During transition, this instinct often backfires.

Energy is limited when work disappears. Not because people have become less capable, but because uncertainty, disrupted routines, and emotional load consume more capacity than is visible. In this state, optimisation demands more than the system can reliably give.

This is why energy comes before optimisation.

Energy is a leading indicator. It tells you what is sustainable and what is not. When energy improves, capacity follows. When energy is ignored, even well-designed plans collapse under their own weight.

Optimisation focuses on how to do more or do better. Energy-focused decision-making asks a different question: does this give me energy, or take more than it returns?

This is not an argument for comfort or avoidance. It is an argument for realism.

Effort that consistently drains energy does not build resilience. It erodes it. Over time, this can lead to burnout disguised as productivity, where people appear active but feel increasingly depleted.

Paying attention to energy helps prevent this.

It encourages selectivity. It invites you to stop polishing things that do not matter yet. It allows you to prioritise actions that restore curiosity, interest, and a sense of aliveness, even if they are not immediately efficient.

This principle also protects against turning recovery into another performance.

When optimisation is prioritised too early, people begin to judge themselves harshly for not doing enough, not moving fast enough, or not using their time "properly". Energy-aware decision-making softens that edge.

It shifts the focus from output to sustainability.

Energy is not static. It fluctuates. Some days will feel lighter than others. The compass does not ask you to optimise every day. It helps you notice patterns over time and adjust accordingly.

If a particular action consistently leaves you drained, it is information. If something restores a sense of engagement or interest, it is information too.

Listening to these signals is not indulgent. It is how momentum is rebuilt without self-betrayal.

Optimisation has its place. So does efficiency.

But during transition, energy is the resource that makes everything else possible. Protect it first.

USING THE COMPASS DAY TO DAY

The Between Chapters Compass is not something you "implement". It is something you return to.

In practice, using the compass day to day is less about following rules and more about asking better questions. It does not demand consistency or discipline. It works even when used briefly, imperfectly, or only when things feel off. Most days, it will show up as a pause.

A moment where you notice pressure building. A decision that feels heavier than it should. A sense that you are pushing, optimising, or second-guessing yourself again.

That pause is the cue.

Instead of asking what the correct move is, the compass invites a small check-in. Not with your long-term goals, but with your current capacity.

You might ask yourself:
- Does this help stabilise me, or does it add strain?
- Does this increase my sense of agency, or reduce it?
- Does this return more energy than it costs?
- Is this movement, or is it another form of waiting?

These are not questions to answer exhaustively. A quick, honest response is usually enough.

Sometimes the compass will confirm that what you are doing makes sense, even if it does not look impressive from the outside. Other times, it will gently highlight a mismatch, a moment where habit or pressure has taken over.

When that happens, the adjustment does not need to be dramatic.

It might mean doing something smaller. Choosing something lower-risk. Letting go of a task that is draining without being useful. Or simply stopping for the day instead of pushing through.

Using the compass does not guarantee smooth progress. It does not remove uncertainty or prevent mistakes. What it does is reduce unnecessary self-conflict.

It helps you distinguish between discomfort that comes from growth and discomfort that comes from misalignment. It allows you to move without constantly judging whether you are doing enough, fast enough, or correctly.

Over time, this has a quiet cumulative effect. Decisions take less effort. You recover more quickly from missteps. You trust yourself a little more.

The compass becomes a familiar reference point, something you can return to whenever the noise increases or clarity fades again.

You will not use it every day. You will forget it sometimes.

That is not a failure. It is part of the process.

The value of the compass lies not in perfect application, but in repeated return. Each time you orient yourself, even briefly, you reinforce the habit of choosing with care rather than reacting under pressure. That is enough.

What This Framework Protects You From

The Between Chapters Compass is useful not only for what it encourages, but for what it quietly prevents.

Periods of transition create a particular kind of vulnerability. When certainty is low and pressure is high, people are more likely to make decisions that feel necessary in the moment but leave them feeling diminished afterwards. Not because they chose badly, but because they chose under strain.

This framework exists to reduce that strain.

One of the first things it protects you from is rushing. Urgency often masquerades as motivation. It tells you that time is running out, that you must decide now, that any pause is a risk. In reality, urgency during transition is rarely accurate. It is more often a response to discomfort than to real deadlines.

The compass helps you slow that reflex just enough to choose rather than react.

It also protects you from over-optimising too early. When pressure builds, people often try to refine everything at once. They polish language, perfect plans, and search for the most efficient route forward. This can drain energy quickly, especially when the foundations are still shifting.

By prioritising stability and energy, the framework keeps you from turning recovery into another performance.

Another quiet protection is against self-betrayal. In uncertain moments, it is tempting to agree to things that do not fit, to chase options that feel misaligned, or to present yourself as more certain than you are. These choices may create short-term relief, but they often leave a residue of doubt or resentment.

The compass makes it easier to notice when an action undermines your sense of agency, even if it looks sensible on paper.

It also guards against the false comfort of certainty. Certainty can feel reassuring, but when it is forced, it becomes brittle. Plans made too early tend to collapse, taking confidence with them. By allowing movement without commitment, the framework reduces the risk of tying your sense of self to outcomes you cannot yet control.

Finally, the compass protects you from the quiet erosion of self-trust. Repeatedly overriding your own capacity, ignoring energy signals, or pushing through misalignment can gradually undermine confidence. The framework interrupts that pattern by legitimising care, pacing, and honest assessment.

None of these protections are dramatic. They work in the background. Their effect is cumulative.

Over time, you are less likely to exhaust yourself unnecessarily. Less likely to rush into decisions you later regret. Less likely to lose yourself while trying to move forward.

You are more likely to remain intact. That, in itself, is progress.

CARRYING THIS FORWARD

The Between Chapters Compass is not something to master. It is not a framework you need to remember in detail or apply consistently. It is a way of orienting yourself that can be picked up and put down as needed, returned to whenever the ground feels unstable again.

You will not always use it consciously. Sometimes it will simply shape how a decision feels. Other times it will help you name why something feels off, even if you cannot yet explain it fully.

This framework is designed to travel with you through uncertainty, not to resolve it in one pass. You will revisit these principles in different forms across the rest of this book. Each time, they will meet you in a slightly different place.

You do not need to apply all four principles at once. Often, one will matter more than the others depending on the moment. Stability might be the priority one week. Movement the next. Energy another time.

The compass adapts because you do. As you move forward, you will notice that the urge to over-plan, over-learn, or over-optimise still appears from time to time. That does not mean the framework has failed. It means you are human. Each return to orientation, however brief, reinforces the habit of choosing with care rather than reacting under pressure.

The next chapter takes this one step further, introducing practical ways to translate orientation into behaviour. Not through big commitments or rigid routines, but through small, low-risk practices designed to rebuild momentum gently.

You do not need to feel ready for that yet. You do not need to anticipate what comes next. For now, it is enough to know that you have a way of moving that does not depend on certainty.

You are not lost. You are navigating unfamiliar ground. And you now have something to guide you.

Chapter 5

THE PRACTICES

HOW TO USE THESE PRACTICES

Before looking at any of the practices that follow, it is important to be clear about how this chapter is meant to be used.

These practices are not a programme. They are not a routine. They are not something you need to "keep up".

They exist to help you take small steps during a period when energy, confidence, and clarity may still be limited. Nothing here requires you to feel ready, motivated, or certain.

Each practice is an invitation, not an instruction.

You do not need to do them all. You do not need to do them in order. You do not need to repeat them once you have tried them. One practice, done once, is enough for this chapter to have done its job.

All of the practices follow the same basic rules.

No practice should take more than thirty to forty-five minutes. None require perfect conditions. Everything is optional.

If you begin something and decide to stop, that still counts as information, not failure.

These practices are designed as experiments.

You are not committing to a habit or making a promise about the future. You are simply testing what happens when you act in a small, contained way. The outcome is not success or failure. It is data.

Some practices may feel immediately helpful. Others may feel irrelevant or irritating. That does not mean you are doing anything wrong. It simply means not every tool is right for every moment.

If you feel resistance as you read, that is normal.

Resistance usually signals one of two things. Either a practice does not fit where you are right now, or it touches something tender. In both cases, you are free to skip it.

Nothing in this chapter needs to be shared, posted, published, or explained to anyone else. These practices are private by default. They are about rebuilding your relationship with action, not performing progress.

A simple way to choose is to notice what feels most depleted.

If your days feel chaotic, start with a stabilising practice. If you feel powerless, choose something that restores agency. If you feel stuck, try a movement practice. If you feel flat or numb, look for something that reconnects you with energy or curiosity.

You are not trying to fix your life here. You are simply asking one small question: what can I do this week that does not make things worse?

The sections that follow offer a range of answers to that question. Take one. Leave the rest. Return later if it helps. Momentum is rebuilt quietly.

Stabilising Practices

When work disappears, one of the first things to erode is a sense of steadiness.

Days lose their shape. Time stretches or collapses unpredictably. Small decisions begin to carry more weight than they should, not because they are important, but because there is no longer a structure holding them in place. Before confidence, clarity, or momentum can return, some degree of stability needs to be re-established. These practices are designed to do that quietly.

They are not about rebuilding a full routine or recreating the discipline of work. They are about restoring just enough predictability and containment to reduce background strain.

If things currently feel chaotic, unmoored, or harder than they should be, start here.

PRACTICE 1: RECLAIMING A GENTLE DAILY ANCHOR

What this practice helps with

Restoring a sense of predictability and grounding during the day.

When to use it

When your days feel shapeless, scattered, or emotionally noisy. When time seems to slip away or drag unpredictably. When you want a sense of "something solid" without committing to a routine.

The practice

Choose one small, repeatable action that you will do at roughly the same time each day for the next few days.

This is not a habit. It is not a productivity tool. It is simply an anchor.

Good anchors are:
- simple
- low effort
- independent of motivation

Examples include:
- making the same drink first thing in the morning
- taking a short walk at a similar time each day
- closing the day by writing in a notebook

The action itself does not matter much. What matters is that it is:

- predictable
- contained
- easy to complete

Do not improve it. Do not extend it. Do not optimise it.

If it takes more than a few minutes, it is too much.

Reflection

After a few days, notice:

- Does the day feel slightly more contained?
- Is there a moment where you feel a little more settled?
- Does time feel marginally less chaotic?

You are not looking for transformation. You are looking for a small reduction in friction.

When to stop

You can stop this practice:

- after one day
- after a few days
- whenever it stops feeling useful

If it becomes effortful, let it go.

The anchor has done its job if it helped you feel even slightly more grounded.

Why this works

Stability is not created by doing more. It is created by making fewer things predictable.

This practice gives your nervous system one reliable reference point. That alone can reduce the sense that everything is in flux.

You are not rebuilding your life here. You are simply giving the day a place to land.

PRACTICE 2: REDUCING INVISIBLE DRAINS

What this practice helps with

Freeing up energy by removing or softening something that is quietly exhausting you.

When to use it

When you feel tired without having done very much. When your days feel heavier than they should. When it feels as though energy is leaking away, but you cannot quite say where.

The practice

Invisible drains are small, ongoing sources of friction that consume energy without producing anything useful in return.

They are often overlooked because they have become normal.

Set aside twenty to thirty minutes for this practice.

1. Take a piece of paper or open a blank note.
2. Write the heading: "Things that quietly drain me right now."
3. Without analysing or judging, list anything that comes to mind.

This might include:
- checking certain apps or feeds out of habit
- checking job boards
- leaving emails or messages unanswered because they feel heavy
- background news consumption
- an unresolved task that keeps tugging at your attention
- a conversation you keep replaying
- a commitment that no longer fits

Do not aim for completeness. Five items is enough.

Now choose one item from the list and decide how you will reduce it, not eliminate it entirely.

Reduction might mean:
- checking something once a day instead of repeatedly
- muting notifications temporarily
- deciding not to decide about something this week
- writing down a worry so it stops looping
- explicitly postponing a decision

The goal is not to solve the issue. It is to stop paying for it repeatedly.

Make the smallest adjustment that reduces friction.

Reflection

After a day or two, notice:
- Does your head feel slightly quieter?
- Is there a small increase in available energy?
- Does one less thing feel like it is pulling at you?

If the effect is barely noticeable, that is fine. Invisible drains are removed quietly.

When to stop

You can stop this practice:
- as soon as the adjustment is made
- if it starts to feel complicated
- if you find yourself trying to optimise it

This is a one-off intervention, not a system.

Why this works

When work disappears, uncertainty already consumes more energy than usual. Invisible drains add to that load without offering anything back.

Removing just one source of friction can create a disproportionate sense of relief. Not because life is suddenly easier, but because your system has one less thing to manage.

You are not trying to become efficient. You are trying to become lighter. That is enough for now.

PRACTICE 3: THE "ENOUGH FOR TODAY" CLOSE

What this practice helps with

Creating a clear end to the day and reducing the feeling that you should always be doing more.

When to use it

When days feel endless or undefined. When you struggle to stop thinking about what you should be doing. When rest feels uneasy or undeserved.

The practice

When work disappears, the day often loses its natural endpoint.

There is no commute, no handover, no obvious signal that it is time to stop. Without that boundary, effort can stretch on indefinitely, even when it is no longer productive. This practice restores a sense of closure.

Choose a time in the late afternoon or early evening. The exact time doesn't matter; what matters is that it is deliberate.

Set aside five to ten minutes.

1. Pause whatever you are doing.
2. Take a piece of paper or open a blank note.
3. Write the heading: "Enough for today."
4. Under it, list three things you did that count as effort.

These do not need to be impressive. They do not need to be productive in the traditional sense.

They might include:
- getting out of bed on a difficult day
- taking a walk
- making a phone call you were avoiding
- trying one of the practices in this book
- noticing that you needed rest

Once the list is complete, read it back to yourself. Then stop.

Do not add tasks. Do not plan tomorrow. Do not evaluate the day.

The act of naming "enough" is the close.

Reflection

Over a few days, notice:
- Does it feel easier to disengage in the evening?
- Does rest feel slightly less loaded with guilt?
- Does the day feel more complete, even if little changed?

You are not aiming for satisfaction. You are aiming for containment.

When to stop

You can stop this practice:

- after one day
- when it begins to feel repetitive
- or whenever evenings start to feel more settled

If you forget to do it, nothing breaks.

Why this works

Without an endpoint, the mind assumes there is still something unresolved. This keeps you in a low-level state of vigilance, even during rest.

Declaring "enough" gives the day a boundary. It tells your system that, for now, nothing more is required.

You are not closing the door on the future. You are simply closing the door on today. That is allowed.

AGENCY-BUILDING PRACTICES

Once a little stability has returned, the next thing to rebuild is agency.

Agency is not confidence. It is not clarity. It is not ambition. Agency is the experience of choosing.

When work disappears, agency often erodes quietly. Decisions feel heavier. Options feel narrower. It can begin to feel as though life is happening to you, rather than something you are participating in.

These practices are designed to reverse that feeling gently.

They are not about outcomes. They are about restoring the sense that you still have influence over your actions, even in small ways.

If you are feeling powerless, hesitant, or as though you are waiting for permission, start here.

PRACTICE 4: ONE CHOSEN ACTION

What this practice helps with

Rebuilding the experience of deliberate choice, independent of outcome.

When to use it

When you feel reactive rather than intentional. When days pass without a clear sense of having decided anything. When motivation feels unreliable, but you want to feel less passive.

The practice

Set aside fifteen to twenty minutes.

Choose one small action you will take today because you chose it, not because it is urgent, expected, or impressive.

This action should be:

- low risk
- achievable today
- complete in itself

Examples include:

- sending a message you have been avoiding
- spending time thinking about something that interests you
- saying no to something that does not fit

What matters is not what you choose, but that the choice is conscious.

Before you do the action, pause and say (silently or out loud): "I am choosing to do this." Then do it.

Stop when the action is complete. Do not extend it. Do not add more.

Reflection

Afterwards, notice:

- Does it feel different from tasks you do out of obligation?
- Is there a small sense of ownership or relief?
- Does it remind you that choice is still available?

You are not looking for satisfaction. You are looking for agency.

When to stop

You can stop this practice:

- after one action
- if you forget to do it
- if it starts to feel performative

This practice works even once.

Why this works

Agency is rebuilt through experience, not affirmation.

Choosing one small action reminds you that you are still an active participant in your life. Even when circumstances are constrained, choice remains.

You do not need to choose something important. You only need to choose something deliberately. That is enough to begin.

Practice 5: The Small Decision Rehearsal

What this practice helps with

Reducing decision fatigue and restoring confidence in your ability to choose.

When to use it

When even small decisions feel heavier than they should. When you find yourself second-guessing or deferring choices. When you feel hesitant to decide without certainty.

The practice

During periods of uncertainty, the cost of deciding can feel inflated.

You may notice yourself delaying simple choices, not because they matter, but because decision-making itself has begun to feel risky. This practice reduces that load by rehearsing decisions where the outcome does not matter.

Set aside ten to fifteen minutes.

1. Identify three low-stakes decisions you can make today.
2. For each one, choose quickly and deliberately.
3. Once chosen, do not revisit or revise it.

Examples of low-stakes decisions:
- what to eat or drink
- when to take a break
- which task to do first

If you notice yourself overthinking, pause and choose anyway. The key is not choosing well. It is choosing without escalation.

Reflection

After the decisions are made, notice:
- Did anything go wrong?
- Did the outcome matter as much as it felt like it might?
- Does deciding feel slightly less threatening now?

You are training your system to experience choice as safe again.

When to stop

You can stop this practice:
- after one round
- once decisions feel easier
- or as soon as it begins to feel forced

This is a rehearsal, not a discipline.

Why this works

Confidence in decision-making does not return through thinking about better choices. It returns through repeated experiences of choosing and surviving the result.

Low-stakes decisions create that experience without risk.

You are not practising decisiveness for its own sake. You are reminding yourself that choosing does not require certainty. That reminder is often enough.

Movement Without Exposure

For many people, the hardest part of taking action during transition is not the action itself. It is the exposure.

Movement is often framed as something public. Updating profiles. Reaching out. Announcing intentions. Being visible before you feel ready. For someone who is still stabilising, this can feel overwhelming.

These practices remove that pressure.

They are designed to help you move privately, without an audience, without explanation, and without the sense that every action is a signal about who you are or where you are going.

If you feel stuck but wary of being seen, start here.

PRACTICE 6: PRIVATE CONTRIBUTION

What this practice helps with

Restoring a sense of usefulness and contribution without visibility.

When to use it

When you want to feel productive but not performative. When the idea of "putting yourself out there" feels too much. When you miss the feeling of contributing something real.

The practice

Set aside twenty to thirty minutes.

Choose one small thing you can do that would be useful to someone, even if they never see it.

This might be:
- drafting an idea or solution for a problem you care about
- improving a document for your future self
- preparing something that could be shared later, but doesn't have to be

The key is that the work is real, but the audience is optional. Do not publish it. Do not send it. Do not seek feedback. Once the time is up, stop.

Reflection

Afterwards, notice:

- Does it feel different from passive consumption?
- Is there a small sense of having contributed rather than prepared?
- Does usefulness feel safer than visibility?

You are not aiming for recognition. You are reconnecting with contribution.

When to stop

You can stop this practice:

- after one session
- if it starts to feel like work-for-work's-sake
- or if you find yourself wanting to polish it

The value is in doing, not in finishing.

Why this works

Contribution is one of the fastest ways to restore confidence, but only when it does not require performance.

Private contribution allows you to act, create, and help without triggering fear of judgement. It reminds you that you still have something to offer, even if you are not ready to show it yet. That reminder matters.

Practice 7: Using What You Already Know

What this practice helps with

Restoring confidence by applying existing knowledge or skills, rather than acquiring more.

When to use it

When you feel tempted to learn more instead of act. When you know a lot but feel strangely hesitant to use it. When preparation has started to replace participation.

The practice

Set aside twenty to thirty minutes.

Choose one thing you already know how to do reasonably well.

This could be:

- a professional skill you have used before
- a way of thinking or problem-solving you are good at
- a process you understand deeply
- an area where people often ask for your input

Now use that knowledge or skill once, in a small, contained way.

Examples include:

- explaining a concept clearly in writing, just for yourself
- sketching a solution to a familiar problem
- improving something small using skills you already have
- outlining advice you would give if someone asked

Do not research. Do not refresh your knowledge. Do not check whether you are doing it "right".

The point is to apply what you already carry, not to top it up. Stop when the time is up.

Reflection

Afterwards, notice:

- Did the skill come back more easily than expected?
- Did you feel more capable once you started?
- Did action reduce the sense of doubt, even slightly?

You are not trying to prove anything. You are reminding yourself that competence does not disappear.

When to stop

You can stop this practice:

- after one use
- if you notice yourself slipping back into preparation
- or when the action feels complete enough

There is no need to turn this into a project.

Why this works

During transition, it is easy to believe that you need to update, retrain, or requalify before you are allowed to act again. This practice challenges that assumption.

Most people already know far more than they are currently using. Applying that knowledge, even briefly, restores trust in your own capability.

You are not starting from zero. You never were.

CONFIDENCE THROUGH USE

Confidence is often misunderstood as a feeling you wait for.

In reality, confidence is a relationship. It is the trust you have in your ability to act and respond, even when outcomes are uncertain. When work disappears, that relationship can weaken, not because ability is lost, but because it is no longer being exercised.

These practices are designed to rebuild confidence through use.

They do not ask you to believe anything new about yourself. They create small experiences that provide evidence. Evidence that you can act, adapt, and recover, even when conditions are imperfect.

If you feel capable in theory but hesitant in practice, start here.

PRACTICE 8: THE LOW-RISK TEST

What this practice helps with

Rebuilding confidence by treating action as experimentation, not commitment.

When to use it

When you feel stuck because outcomes feel too final. When fear of getting it wrong is blocking movement. When you want to act but without consequences.

The practice

Set aside twenty to thirty minutes.

Choose one small action that meets all three of these conditions:

- it is reversible
- it is low visibility
- it will produce information, not judgement

Examples include:

- testing a new way of approaching a familiar task
- drafting something you do not have to send
- reaching out informally to ask a question, not make a request
- trying a different structure for something you already do

Before you begin, say to yourself: "This is a test, not a decision." Then do the action.

Once complete, stop. Do not escalate. Do not optimise.

Reflection

Afterwards, ask:
- What did I learn?
- Was the outcome survivable?
- Did acting feel less risky than waiting?

You are not evaluating success. You are collecting evidence.

When to stop

You can stop this practice:
- after one test
- when the action begins to feel heavier
- or when you feel tempted to turn it into a plan

A single test is enough.

Why this works

Confidence grows when action stops being treated as a referendum on your worth.

Low-risk tests allow you to engage with uncertainty without staking your identity on the outcome. They rebuild trust by showing that you can act, observe, and adjust. That trust accumulates quietly.

PRACTICE 9: EVIDENCE CAPTURE

What this practice helps with

Strengthening confidence by recording proof of competence before doubt erases it.

When to use it

When you forget what you are capable of. When doubt returns quickly after small successes. When your internal narrative feels harsher than the evidence.

The practice

During periods of uncertainty, confidence often suffers from a memory problem.

What you did yesterday fades. What you struggled with today feels larger. Without intention, your internal story becomes skewed towards doubt.

This practice corrects that imbalance.

Set aside ten minutes.
1. Take a notebook or open a document.
2. Create a heading: "Evidence."
3. Write down three things that demonstrate competence, capability, or effort.

These might include:
- something you handled reasonably well
- a small action you took despite resistance
- a problem you understood or clarified
- a skill you used without thinking

They do not need to be impressive. They only need to be true.

If this feels difficult, start smaller:
- I finished something.
- I showed up.
- I tried.

Once written, stop.

Do not analyse. Do not qualify. Do not downplay.

Reflection

Return to this list later and notice:
- Does it challenge the story you tell yourself?
- Does it make doubt feel less convincing?
- Does it remind you that capability is still present?

You are not trying to feel confident. You are reminding yourself of what is already happening.

When to stop

You can stop this practice:
- after one entry
- when it starts to feel repetitive
- or whenever the list feels complete enough

You do not need to maintain it daily.

Why this works

Confidence erodes not because ability disappears, but because evidence is forgotten.

Capturing proof interrupts that pattern. It gives your future self something solid to refer to when doubt resurfaces.

You are not collecting achievements. You are preserving perspective. That is often enough.

ENERGY AND CURIOSITY

After disruption, it is common to go looking for purpose.

This search often carries too much weight. Purpose is expected to arrive fully formed, to explain everything, and to motivate sustained action. When it does not, people conclude that something is wrong with them.

This section takes a different approach.

Before purpose, before passion, before direction, there is energy.

Energy is a quieter signal. It shows up as interest, mild curiosity, or a subtle sense of engagement. It does not shout. It does not demand commitment. It simply pulls your attention slightly towards something.

These practices invite you to notice and follow that pull, without explanation or pressure.

If you feel flat, numb, or disconnected from what once mattered, start here.

PRACTICE 10: FOLLOWING A LIGHT PULL

What this practice helps with

Reconnecting with energy and interest without forcing meaning or outcomes.

When to use it

When nothing feels particularly motivating. When you are tired of asking yourself what you "should" care about. When you want to feel a little more alive, without pressure.

The practice

Set aside twenty to thirty minutes.

Think back over the last few days and notice anything that caught your attention, even briefly.

This might be:

- a topic you lingered on
- an idea that stayed with you
- a question you found yourself returning to
- something you enjoyed more than expected

Choose one of these and spend a short period engaging with it.

Engagement might look like:
- reading a little more about it
- writing down your thoughts
- experimenting with it in a small way
- talking it through, even just with yourself

Do not justify the choice. Do not ask where it leads. Do not turn it into a plan.

Follow the pull, lightly. Stop when the time is up.

Reflection

Afterwards, notice:
- Did time pass differently?
- Did the activity feel less draining?
- Did interest appear without effort?

You are not looking for passion. You are noticing energy.

When to stop

You can stop this practice:
- after one session
- when curiosity fades
- or when it starts to feel effortful

Curiosity is fragile. Let it go when it wants to.

Why this works

Energy often returns before clarity.

By following small pulls rather than forcing purpose, you allow interest to re-emerge naturally. Over time, these signals can form the beginnings of direction, but only if they are not burdened with expectation.

You are not deciding what matters yet. You are noticing what still responds. That is enough for now.

Choosing One, Then Stopping

By the time you reach the end of this chapter, it may feel as though there is a lot here. That is not an instruction to do more.

This chapter is not asking you to become disciplined, consistent, or productive. It is asking you to choose one small thing, try it, and then stop.

If you are unsure where to begin, let how you feel guide you. If your days feel chaotic, choose a stabilising practice. If you feel powerless, choose an agency practice. If you feel stuck, choose a movement practice. If you feel flat, choose an energy practice.

There is no correct choice. Any one of them is enough. You do not need to repeat a practice to make it count. You do not need to combine them. You do not need to notice immediate results. Momentum at this stage is often quiet and internal.

What matters is that you have acted once, deliberately and without pressure. That single act is already a change. If you try a practice and nothing shifts, that is still information. If you stop halfway through, that counts too. The point is not completion, but contact. You are rebuilding trust in your ability to act without being driven by urgency or fear.

You may notice that after taking a small step, your language begins to shift. The way you describe yourself, your situation, and your options may start to change, even before anything external does. That is not an accident. Action reshapes narrative.

The next chapter looks at what it means to rebuild a sense of identity without rushing to replace what has been lost, and how to carry continuity forward even when roles have ended.

For now, stop here. You have done enough.

Chapter 6

REBUILDING IDENTITY WITHOUT RUSHING IT

THE QUIET FEAR UNDERNEATH CHANGE

Most people think the hardest part of transition is practical.

They worry about income, timing, or what comes next. Those concerns are real, but they are rarely the deepest source of unease. Beneath them sits something quieter and more unsettling. A question that is rarely spoken out loud: who am I if I'm not that person anymore?

Work does more than pay the bills. It provides structure, rhythm, and a steady stream of signals about who we are in the world. It tells us where to go, what to focus on, and how we are seen. When that structure loosens or disappears, it is not just routines that fall away. Identity wobbles.

This is why periods between chapters can feel strangely disorienting, even for capable, experienced people. You may still know what you are good at. You may still have skills, insight, and judgement. And yet, when someone asks a simple question like "So, what do you do?", the answer no longer comes easily.

The discomfort that follows is often misunderstood. People assume it means they have lost confidence, direction, or relevance. In reality, it is the nervous system reacting to the sudden absence of familiar signals. When labels drop away, the mind scrambles to find footing.

Silence amplifies this. Without meetings, deadlines, or feedback loops, there are fewer daily reminders of competence. Without a clear role, comparison creeps in. You may find yourself measuring your progress against others who appear to be moving forward, even if you know nothing about their internal experience.

This combination can create a quiet but persistent fear. Not a dramatic panic, but a low-level sense of unease. A worry that if this phase goes on too long, something essential will erode. That you will drift. That you will be forgotten. That you will lose momentum you may never regain.

It is important to say this clearly. This fear is not a sign that something has gone wrong. It is a natural response to identity being in motion without yet having new language to stabilise it. You are not in freefall. You are in transition. There is a difference.

Freefall implies loss of control and direction. Transition implies movement between known states. One is chaotic. The other is simply incomplete.

The discomfort you are feeling is not evidence of collapse. It is evidence that something is changing, and that the old structures no longer fully apply. Naming this matters.

When the fear remains unspoken, it tends to shape behaviour indirectly. People rush into decisions, over-commit to explanations, or cling to outdated labels because they want the unease to stop. The urge to "sort it out" becomes stronger than the need to let it settle.

This chapter takes a different approach.

Rather than trying to eliminate the fear, it helps you understand it, contain it, and move through it without rushing to replace one identity with another.

You are not losing yourself. You are temporarily without a label that used to do some of the work for you.

The sections that follow focus on separating identity from role, restoring continuity beneath change, and helping you hold a sense of self that allows you to be unfinished without feeling diminished.

For now, it is enough to recognise this, if you feel unsettled, it is not because you are failing, it is because you are between versions of yourself.

That is a place many capable people pass through, even if few talk about it openly.

IDENTITY IS NOT THE SAME AS ROLE

One of the quiet assumptions modern work encourages is that identity and role are interchangeable.

Ask someone who they are, and they will often answer with a job title. Ask how they are doing, and the state of their work tends to dominate the response. Over time, this shorthand becomes normalised, not because it is accurate, but because it is convenient.

During transition, that convenience disappears. When a role ends or loosens, the identity that leaned on it can feel suddenly unsupported. People describe this as feeling "lost", even when nothing essential about them has actually gone.

This is where a distinction becomes important. A role is a container. Identity is the pattern that shows up inside it.

Roles define where you apply yourself. They describe scope, authority, and context. They are shaped by organisations, markets, and timing. They can be created, altered, and removed without reference to who you are as a person.

Identity, by contrast, is portable. It is carried in how you think, how you respond under pressure, how you make sense of complexity, how you treat others, and what you consistently care about. These things persist even when the environment changes.

Confusing role with identity is understandable. Work occupies a large portion of life, and roles come with strong social signals. Titles offer a quick way to locate ourselves and be located by others. But when identity is outsourced to role, it becomes fragile.

This is why the loss or change of work can feel so destabilising. It is not just the role that has gone. The shorthand that made identity legible has gone with it.

Rebuilding stability begins by separating what has ended from what remains. One way to do this is to name different layers explicitly:

- There is the role you occupied: where and how you applied yourself.
- There are your capabilities: what you brought, repeatedly and reliably.
- There are your values: what you would not trade, even under pressure.
- And there is your character: how you show up when things are uncertain.

The role may change or disappear. The other layers do not vanish with it.

During transition, it can be grounding to speak to yourself from this distinction:
- My role ended. My capabilities didn't.
- A title is a container, not a definition.
- I am not 'nothing' between jobs, I am temporarily unlabelled.

This is not positive thinking. It is accurate thinking. When you hold identity at the level of capability, values, and character, continuity becomes easier to see. You are no longer measuring yourself against a missing label. You are noticing what still travels with you.

This also shifts how you interpret the discomfort of transition. Feeling untethered does not mean you lack substance. It means the usual signposts are gone, and new ones have not yet been installed. That is a structural issue, not a personal one.

As the chapter unfolds, this distinction becomes more than conceptual. It gives you a way to think about yourself without clinging to old roles or rushing into new ones. It creates space for evolution without erasure.

Continuity Is Real, Even When the Story Feels Broken

One of the most unsettling aspects of transition is the sense that your story has snapped. What once felt like a coherent progression now looks fragmented. The past feels oddly distant, the future unclear, and the present hard to describe. It can feel as though the thread that held everything together has been lost.

This feeling is powerful, but it is not the full picture. What often breaks during transition is not continuity itself, but the story you were using to make sense of it. When the narrative structure disappears, it can seem as though the substance has gone with it.

In reality, continuity is carried in quieter places. It lives in patterns rather than positions. If you look beneath roles and timelines, you will often find the same themes repeating. The same kinds of problems that draw you in. The same ways you tend to contribute when things matter. The same standards you hold yourself to, even when circumstances change.

These patterns do not vanish when a role ends. They persist through pauses, pivots, and periods of uncertainty. They are harder to see when there are fewer external markers, but they are still there.

This is why people often feel more disoriented than incapable during transition. The internal sense of self is intact, but the external signals that reflected it back have gone quiet. Without meetings, deadlines, or recognition, it becomes harder to see yourself in action. The mirror is missing, not the person. Recognising this can be stabilising.

Continuity shows up in at least four places:

- In strengths, which tend to repeat regardless of context. You may find yourself once again making sense of complexity, supporting others through uncertainty, or bringing order where things are messy.
- In values, which continue to guide what feels acceptable or draining. Even without a role, you will notice when something aligns with what you care about and when it does not.
- In contribution style, the way you naturally help. Some people steady situations. Some challenge assumptions. Some connect people. Some build systems. These tendencies persist across environments.
- And in relationships, particularly in who still reaches out to you and why. Trust does not disappear when a job ends. It is built on how you show up, not where you sit.

These are not conclusions yet. They're evidence.

When the story feels broken, it can help to look for these signals rather than trying to repair the narrative immediately. You do not need to explain your career to prove continuity. You need to notice where it is already present.

This reframing also softens the pressure to "get back on track". There is no single track you have fallen off. There is a pattern that is continuing to express itself, even if the setting has changed. Seeing that pattern restores a sense of self without requiring you to decide what comes next.

It can be helpful to remind yourself:
- I haven't disappeared, I'm recalibrating.
- The thread is still there, even if the plot is unclear.
- This is a pause in the story, not the end of it.

As continuity becomes easier to recognise, the idea of "starting again" begins to lose its grip.

You Are Not Starting Again, You're Evolving

One of the most common phrases people use during transition is, "It feels like I'm starting again."

It is an understandable feeling, but it is rarely an accurate description.

What usually gets labelled as "starting over" is the experience of being temporarily without a clear role, structure, or destination. The familiar markers that once signalled progress have gone quiet, and without them it can feel as though everything has reset.

But very little has actually been erased.

You have not lost your judgement. You have not lost your ability to read situations. You have not lost the experience of what has worked and what has not. You have not lost the relationships, instincts, or resilience built over time.

Those things do not vanish when a job ends or a direction changes.

What is happening instead is evolution.

Evolution involves carrying forward what still fits, releasing what no longer does, and updating how you describe yourself to match reality. It is not a return to zero. It is a continuation, with adjustment.

The language of "starting again" can be unhelpful because it implies a blank slate where none exists. It suggests that previous effort no longer counts, and that you must re-earn legitimacy from the beginning. This framing creates unnecessary pressure and often leads people to rush.

When you recognise this phase as evolution, the pressure shifts.

You are not required to recreate yourself. You are not obliged to abandon your past to justify your future. You are allowed to refine rather than reinvent.

This also changes how you interpret uncertainty.

Not knowing exactly where this leads does not mean you are lost. It means the shape is still forming. Evolution is rarely linear or obvious from the inside. It involves testing, sensing, and adjusting, often without a clear endpoint in view.

You may notice that some aspects of your previous identity feel heavier than they used to. Certain responsibilities, environments, or ways of working may no longer fit as well. Letting those go is not failure. It is information.

At the same time, other aspects may feel more solid than ever. Patterns of contribution, ways of thinking, or values may feel increasingly non-negotiable. These are the elements being carried forward.

It can help to use language that reflects this truth:
- I'm not starting over, I'm starting from experience.
- This is a recalibration, not a reset.
- I'm carrying the skills forward, not the title.

When you speak to yourself this way, the ground feels steadier. You are no longer measuring yourself against an imagined zero point. You are acknowledging continuity while allowing for change.

PERMISSION TO BE UNFINISHED

One of the quiet pressures people feel during transition is the belief that they should be further along by now.

That if enough time has passed, they ought to have clarity. That uncertainty is something to tolerate briefly, not inhabit. When answers do not arrive quickly, unfinishedness can start to feel like failure.

This belief is understandable, but it is not helpful.

Periods of transition are, by definition, incomplete. They involve movement without full visibility. Expecting certainty too early often creates more instability, not less.

Permission to be unfinished changes the relationship you have with this phase.

It does not mean giving up or drifting indefinitely. It means allowing understanding to emerge through experience rather than forcing it into existence through pressure.

When people rush identity, they tend to lock themselves into brittle stories. They choose labels that feel safe rather than true. They over-commit to paths that quiet anxiety but later require undoing. In the long run, this often creates more disruption than taking the time to let things settle.

Being unfinished, by contrast, keeps options open.

It allows you to act, experiment, and learn without declaring conclusions you may soon outgrow. It makes it easier to adjust course as new information appears. It preserves integrity by aligning language with reality.

This chapter has returned to a few themes repeatedly:
- that identity is larger than role
- that continuity exists beneath change
- that evolution is not the same as starting again

Permission to be unfinished is what allows those ideas to be lived, not just understood.

It also connects directly back to the practices you have already explored:
- small actions taken without pressure
- movement without exposure
- confidence built through use, not assertion

All of these rely on the same principle: you do not need to know where something leads in order to take the next step.

Unfinished does not mean ungrounded.

You can be steady without being settled. You can be capable without being defined. You can be moving without being certain.

If you find yourself wanting this chapter to resolve more cleanly, that is worth noticing. The desire for closure often signals fatigue, not readiness. Clarity tends to arrive after movement has had time to do its work.

For now, it is enough to hold this position:

- I am allowed to be unfinished.
- I am not late.
- I am still myself.

The next chapter explores how to talk about yourself during transition, not by returning to old labels or forcing a polished story, but by representing who you are now, honestly and with integrity.

Chapter 7

TELLING YOUR STORY

WHY THE CV BREAKS DOWN DURING TRANSITION

The CV is not a bad tool. It is simply a tool designed for a different moment than the one you are in now.

CVs work best when careers are stable and linear. They compress the past into a clean sequence of roles, responsibilities, and achievements. They assume continuity. They reward clarity of direction and consistency of narrative.

During transition, those assumptions break down. When work disappears, or when you are between chapters, the identity you are carrying is still forming, and the story you are living no longer fits neatly into a linear format. Identity is shifting. Priorities are being reassessed. The next role may not yet be defined. Asking a CV to capture this moment accurately is asking it to do something it was never designed to do.

This is why working on a CV during transition often feels frustrating or draining. You may find yourself trying to force coherence where it does not yet exist. Polishing bullet points while feeling increasingly disconnected from the story they tell. Editing language to sound certain when certainty is exactly what is missing.

The discomfort that arises is often misinterpreted. People assume they are struggling because they lack confidence, clarity, or direction. In reality, the problem is structural. The CV demands a level of resolution that this phase has not yet reached.

CVs also privilege outcomes over process. They highlight titles, timelines, and completed achievements. They are not good at capturing learning, exploration, or partial movement. They struggle with pauses, pivots, and periods of recalibration, even when those periods are meaningful.

This can create a subtle sense of inadequacy. Gaps feel like failures rather than transitions. Provisional steps feel like distractions rather than signals. The signals that matter most during transition – strengths, values, contribution – are flattened or ignored.

None of this means you should abandon your CV forever. It means the CV is not the right place to start.

Trying to update it too early can lock you into an old version of yourself, one that no longer fits but still carries authority because it looks complete and professional.

A different approach is needed at this stage: one that focuses on representation rather than resolution. One that allows you to describe who you are now, without pretending that the future is already decided.

That is what the rest of this chapter introduces. Not a rejection of the CV, but a way to step beyond it, temporarily, while you learn how to represent who you are now – honestly, provisionally, and without pretending the story is finished.

IDENTITY HAS MOVED, EVEN IF LANGUAGE HASN'T

As the previous chapter explored, identity often shifts before it settles. What tends to lag behind is not capability or direction, but language.

During transition, you may sense that something about how you think, work, or relate to problems has changed. You respond differently to situations you once took for granted. Certain roles or labels feel less compelling. You find yourself drawn to problems rather than positions. And yet, when you try to describe this shift, the old language still shows up.

Titles fit awkwardly. Past roles dominate the story. Familiar phrases no longer feel quite true. This does not mean nothing has changed. It means your experience has moved faster than your vocabulary.

Language usually updates after action, not before it. Identity rarely announces itself in a single, clean moment. It evolves through reflection, through small steps taken without certainty, and through noticing what now energises or drains you. Often, the most significant changes are felt before they can be named.

This is where discomfort can arise. When you rely on outdated language to describe a changing identity, conversations can start to feel rehearsed. Written profiles feel hollow. You may struggle to "sell yourself", not because you lack value, but because the story you are telling no longer matches how you experience yourself.

That mismatch is not a failure. It is information. It tells you that identity has moved, and that your language has not yet caught up. Crucially, you do not need to resolve that movement before you speak. You do not need a finished version of who you are becoming. You need a way of representing yourself that allows for motion.

The steps you have already taken, however modest they felt at the time, have begun to update your sense of self. Language will follow, but only if you allow it to remain provisional rather than forcing it into premature certainty. At this point, the problem is not confidence or clarity. It is fit.

The CV is designed to compress the past into a stable, linear story. During transition, that compression can work against you. It asks for certainty where none yet exists, and completeness where honesty would be more useful. What's needed instead is a way of representing yourself that can hold movement, not eliminate it.

What a Showcase Is (And Is Not)

A showcase is not a replacement for a CV. It is a different way of representing yourself when the old format no longer fits.

Where a CV compresses the past into a linear story, a showcase holds the present more lightly. It is designed to show how you think, what you can do, and where your attention is now, without pretending that everything is settled.

A showcase is not a single document with a fixed structure. At its core, it is a collection of signals that help others understand your capabilities and interests without forcing you into a definitive narrative.

At its simplest, a showcase does three things:
- it makes your strengths visible
- it provides evidence of how you work
- it hints at what you are drawn towards now

What a showcase is not is just as important. It is not a personal brand performance. It is not a polished pitch for a role you are not sure you want. It is not a declaration of long-term intent. You are not required to be aspirational, inspirational, or certain.

A showcase is also not a portfolio in the traditional sense. Portfolios tend to assume finished work, clear outcomes, and a defined audience. A showcase can include fragments, experiments, and in-progress thinking. It values signal over completion.

This is what makes it particularly useful during transition.

A showcase allows you to represent who you are now, not who you were, and not who you think you should become. It creates space for honesty without vagueness, and for confidence without over-claiming.

Importantly, a showcase is modular. You can add to it, remove from it, or emphasise different elements depending on context. It evolves as your understanding deepens and your direction clarifies, without locking you into a single story.

If a CV asks you to present certainty, a showcase allows you to present capability. And during transition, capability is the most truthful signal you have.

Shifting the Centre of Gravity

One of the reasons CVs feel so brittle during transition is that they place the centre of gravity in the wrong place.

They ask you to anchor your value in roles, titles, and timelines. They privilege what you were employed to do over what you are actually capable of doing. When work disappears, that anchor disappears with it.

A showcase shifts the centre of gravity elsewhere. Instead of asking, "What was your last role?", it asks, "What do you reliably bring?" This shift is subtle, but it changes everything.

Roles are context-specific. Titles are granted. Timelines are external. Capabilities, by contrast, travel with you. They show up across different environments, problems, and phases of work. They persist even when circumstances change.

When you begin to describe yourself through capabilities rather than positions, the narrative becomes more resilient. This does not mean ignoring your past roles. It means treating them as evidence, not identity. Roles become containers in which capability was expressed, rather than definitions of who you are.

For example, instead of leading with:
- I was a Senior Project Manager at...

You might begin with:
- I'm someone people rely on to bring order to complex work...

The role becomes supporting detail, not the headline.

This shift also reframes gaps and transitions. When value is tied to continuous employment, pauses feel like absences. When value is tied to capability, pauses become context, not commentary. What matters is not whether you were in role, but whether the capability still exists and is being exercised.

The practices in the previous chapter were designed to help you surface exactly this kind of signal. Through small actions, private contribution, and evidence capture, you have already begun to notice what travels with you between chapters. Those signals now become the raw material of your showcase.

A useful way to think about this shift is to ask different questions.

Not:

- What roles have I held?
- What titles have I earned?
- What is the neatest story?

But:

- What problems do people trust me to handle?
- What kinds of work energise me when I'm at my best?
- What patterns show up again and again in how I contribute?

These questions do not demand certainty about the future. They ask only for honesty about the present and the past. Shifting the centre of gravity in this way does not reduce your credibility. It increases it.

People are far better at recognising capability than they are at interpreting job titles. When you describe what you actually do well, rather than where you last sat, you give others something real to respond to.

The Three Elements of a Personal Showcase

A showcase does not need to be comprehensive to be useful.

In fact, trying to make it complete too early often recreates the same pressure that makes a CV feel uncomfortable during transition. What helps instead is a simple structure that allows you to represent yourself honestly, while leaving room to evolve.

A personal showcase is built from three elements: strengths, evidence, and interests.

These elements work together, but they do not need to be equally developed. You may feel clear about one and uncertain about another. That is normal. The showcase remains useful even when parts of it are provisional.

STRENGTHS

Strengths are not job titles or personality traits. They are patterns of capability that show up reliably across different contexts. They describe how you tend to approach problems, interact with others, or add value when things matter.

Examples of strengths might include:
- making sense of complex information
- bringing structure to ambiguous work
- helping others think more clearly
- noticing risks others overlook

You do not need to claim these as fixed or exceptional. You are simply naming what tends to be true when you are working at your best.

If you are unsure, look for repetition. What do people come to you for? What kinds of problems do you often end up handling? What feels effortful for others but relatively natural for you?

Strengths form the backbone of your showcase. They are what travel with you, regardless of role or setting.

EVIDENCE

Evidence grounds your strengths in reality. It is not proof in a legal sense, but signal that makes your capability legible to others.

Evidence does not need to be dramatic or impressive. It can be simple, concrete, and specific. Small examples are often more convincing than grand claims.

Evidence might include:
- a brief story of a problem you helped solve
- an outcome you contributed to
- a piece of work you created
- feedback you received
- a situation you handled well

Importantly, evidence does not need to be tied to formal employment. Work done independently, informally, or privately still counts if it demonstrates capability.

This is where the practices from the previous chapter come back into view. Private contribution, low-risk tests, and evidence capture all generate material that can feed your showcase.

You are not trying to prove your worth. You are simply making it visible.

INTERESTS

Interests are the most provisional part of the showcase, and often the hardest to name. They are not commitments or goals. They are signals of attention.

They show where your curiosity is currently pulling you, even if you do not yet know what that means.

Examples might include:
- certain types of problems or challenges
- particular industries, themes, or questions
- ways of working that feel more energising
- directions you find yourself reading or thinking about

It is enough to say, "I'm currently interested in..." or "I'm finding myself drawn towards...".

Interests give others a sense of where your energy is going, without locking you into a declared path. They are allowed to be vague, and they are allowed to change.

In a showcase, interests add motion. They signal that you are not static, even if your next step is still forming.

How the Elements Work Together

You do not need to perfect all three elements before using them.

A simple showcase might include:
- a clear sense of strengths
- a small amount of evidence
- lightly stated interests

That is enough.

As you continue to act, experiment, and reflect, these elements will naturally evolve. New evidence will appear. Interests will sharpen or shift. Strengths may become clearer in different contexts.

The structure remains the same. The content changes.

This is what makes a showcase resilient during transition. It allows you to speak honestly about what you bring and where your energy is going, without pretending that the future is already decided.

Writing Without Locking Yourself In

One of the biggest sources of hesitation when updating how you present yourself is the fear of getting it wrong.

People worry that if they write something down, they are committing to it. That if they describe themselves in a particular way, they will be held to it. That if they name an interest or a strength, they are declaring a direction they may later change their mind about.

This fear makes sense. Traditional career language is often final. CVs, profiles, and bios are written as if the story is settled, even when it is not. During transition, that expectation can feel paralysing.

A showcase works differently. It is designed to hold current truth, not permanent identity. This is where provisional language becomes important. Provisional language allows you to speak honestly about where you are without over-claiming or performing certainty.

Small shifts in phrasing can make a significant difference.

Instead of:
- I am a...

You might use:
- I tend to work best when...
- I'm currently focused on...
- Much of my work involves...
- I'm exploring...

These phrases create space. They communicate capability and direction without locking you into a fixed label. They signal how you work, not what you are permanently called.

This approach also applies to interests. You do not need to declare a destination. It is enough to describe a direction of travel. Saying, "I'm interested in how teams adapt during change" is very different from claiming, "I am now a change consultant."

One is honest. The other may be premature. Writing this way does not weaken your story. It strengthens it. People are generally more comfortable engaging with someone who can represent where they are, rather than someone who performs certainty they do not yet feel.

Provisional language also makes updating easier. When your showcase is framed as an evolving representation, changing it feels natural rather than corrective. You are not rewriting history. You are reflecting movement.

This is especially important during periods of experimentation. As you try new things, learn what fits, and discard what does not, your language should be able to move with you. If writing feels heavy or restrictive, it is often a sign that the language is too final for the moment you are in.

A useful check is this: if reading your own description makes you feel constrained, it is probably too fixed; if it makes you feel recognised and open, it is probably about right.

The goal is not to sound impressive. It is to sound like yourself, as you are now.

WHERE A SHOWCASE LIVES

A showcase does not need a dedicated platform to be useful.

One of the advantages of stepping away from a CV during transition is that representation becomes more flexible. You are no longer trying to compress everything into a single, polished document. Instead, you are creating a core set of signals that can appear in different places, at different levels of detail.

Think of your showcase as content, not a container. The same ideas can be expressed in multiple forms depending on context. This reduces pressure and makes the work you do here immediately usable.

A showcase might live in one or more of the following places.

It could be a simple document. A single page that captures your strengths, a few pieces of evidence, and your current interests. This might live in a notes app, a shared document, or a notebook. Its primary audience may be you.

It could inform how you present yourself on professional platforms. Rather than rewriting everything, you might adjust a short summary or "About" section so that capabilities lead and roles support. The language remains provisional, not performative.

It could sit in a personal workspace. Some people prefer a Notion page or a simple personal site where they can collect ideas, examples, and reflections. This does not need to be public. It can be a working space rather than a finished product.

It could exist as conversation notes. Perhaps the most immediate use of a showcase is in conversation. When someone asks what you are doing or what you are looking for, your showcase gives you a way to respond without apology or over-explanation. You are not reciting a CV. You are sharing where you are.

The important point is this: you do not need to duplicate your showcase everywhere.

Create it once, then adapt it lightly. Emphasise different elements depending on who you are speaking to and what the context requires. This keeps representation alive rather than rigid.

It is also worth remembering that a showcase can be private. You are not obliged to publish or announce anything before you are ready. The value lies in clarity and alignment, not in visibility. Sharing can come later, when it feels supportive rather than exposing.

Wherever your showcase lives, it should feel usable, not heavy. If maintaining it starts to feel like work, it is probably doing too much. The aim is to support conversations and decisions, not to become another artefact to manage.

USING YOUR SHOWCASE IN CONVERSATION

One of the quiet benefits of a showcase is how it changes the tone of conversation.

When people rely on a CV to explain themselves, conversations often feel brittle. There is a sense of having to justify gaps, defend choices, or present a coherent story before it truly exists. The focus shifts quickly to outcomes and expectations, rather than understanding.

A showcase softens that dynamic. Because it is capability-focused and provisional by design, it gives you a way to talk about yourself without apology or performance. You are not pitching a finished version of yourself. You are sharing where you are and what you bring.

This changes the pressure in subtle but important ways.

Instead of answering, "So what are you looking for?" with a fixed request, you can respond with something more open:
- I tend to do my best work when I'm helping make sense of complex situations.
- Right now I'm exploring roles where that kind of thinking is useful.

This invites conversation rather than judgement.

Instead of feeling the need to explain a pause or transition, you can shift the centre of gravity back to capability:

- I've been using this time to reconnect with the kind of work that energises me.
- I'm noticing that I'm most engaged when I'm working on...

You are not avoiding the truth. You are framing it in a way that reflects reality rather than defensiveness.

A showcase also changes how you listen. Because you are not trying to land a pitch, you can pay more attention to what the other person is actually saying. Conversations become more exploratory. You are both sensing where there might be alignment, rather than negotiating a predefined outcome.

This changes how professional conversations feel. They become less about asking for something and more about exchanging understanding. Less about proving readiness and more about noticing fit. Often, this leads to more useful connections precisely because it is less forced.

It is worth remembering that not every conversation needs to go anywhere. Using your showcase does not obligate you to pursue every opportunity or respond positively to every suggestion. It gives you language to stay present without committing prematurely.

If a conversation feels misaligned, you can acknowledge that honestly, without closing doors:

- That's interesting, though I'm not sure it's quite right for me at the moment.

That, too, is agency.

Over time, you may notice that conversations feel lighter. You are less preoccupied with how you are coming across and more engaged with what is actually being discussed. This is not because you have perfected your story, but because you are no longer forcing one.

A showcase does not guarantee outcomes. It does something more valuable during transition. It allows you to be yourself, honestly and provisionally, while staying open to what emerges.

LETTING THE SHOWCASE EVOLVE

A showcase is not something you finish. It is something you update as you move.

One of the quiet traps people fall into during transition is trying to lock their representation down too early. They treat new language as if it needs to last, as if changing it later would signal indecision or weakness.

In reality, the opposite is true. A showcase gains strength by evolving.

As you take small actions, follow curiosity, and test ideas in the world, new information appears. Some strengths become clearer. Some interests sharpen. Others fade. This is not a failure of clarity; it is the process of finding it.

Your showcase should reflect that movement.

This is where the orienting principles introduced earlier become useful again. When a piece of language no longer feels right, that is information. When something you once emphasised begins to drain rather than energise, that is information too. Updating your showcase in response is not backtracking. It is alignment.

You are allowed to revise your language as often as you need. Nothing you write now needs to be permanent. You are not carving your identity into stone. You are keeping your representation in step with your experience.

This also reduces pressure around "getting it right". When you know you can change it, you are more likely to start. Provisional language makes action safer. It allows you to engage with the world without feeling that every word commits you to a future you cannot yet see.

Over time, something interesting tends to happen. The more you act, the less effort it takes to describe yourself. Language begins to feel less forced. Patterns become easier to name. Confidence grows quietly, not because you have declared it, but because it is supported by evidence.

Your showcase becomes simpler, not more complex. This is a sign that it is doing its job.

Letting the showcase evolve also protects your integrity. You are not presenting a version of yourself you feel obliged to live up to. You are describing who you are and what you bring, honestly and in motion. That honesty makes engagement more sustainable and decisions easier to live with.

You do not need to rush this. A showcase can be revisited occasionally, adjusted lightly, and left alone for long stretches. It exists to support you, not to demand attention. By the end of this chapter, you should feel less pressure to explain gaps, defend transitions, or force certainty. You now have a way of representing yourself that moves with you, rather than holding you in place.

The next chapter explores how progress shows up during transition, often in ways that are easy to miss if you are only looking for outcomes.

For now, this is enough.

Chapter 8

SIGNALS YOU'RE MAKING PROGRESS

WHY OUTCOME-BASED MEASURES FAIL HERE

When people try to assess whether they are making progress during transition, they usually reach for outcomes:

- a new role
- a clear plan
- certainty about what comes next

These measures make sense in stable phases of life. They are visible, socially recognised, and easy to compare. The problem is that during transition, they arrive last.

Using outcomes as your primary measure at this stage is like checking for harvest before the seeds have been planted. The absence of results does not mean nothing is happening. It means the process is still underway.

This is where many people begin to disqualify themselves too early. They look around and see no tangible change, so they conclude that they are stuck. Days or weeks pass without a decisive event, and the internal narrative quietly shifts from patience to self-criticism:

- I should be further along by now.
- If this was working, something would have happened.
- Maybe I'm just not moving at all.

These thoughts are understandable, but they are based on the wrong indicators.

Transition unfolds in layers. Before outcomes appear, behaviour shifts. Before behaviour stabilises, emotions soften. Before emotions settle, energy returns in small, uneven ways.

If you wait for the final layer to change before acknowledging progress, you will miss the earlier ones entirely.

This creates what feels like stagnation but is actually mismeasurement. You are judging a process by markers that do not belong to it.

Outcome-based thinking also introduces unnecessary urgency. When progress is defined only by visible results, every quiet day feels like a failure. This pressure often leads people to rush decisions, over-commit to explanations, or chase resolution simply to escape the discomfort of not knowing.

In doing so, they undermine the very steadiness that makes meaningful progress possible.

It can help to remember this: outcomes are confirmation, not creation.

They confirm what has already shifted internally and behaviourally. They do not cause it. If you are waiting for an outcome to prove that progress is happening, you are waiting for the last signal rather than the first.

This chapter invites a different approach. Instead of asking, "What has resolved?", it asks, "What has changed?"

The sections that follow focus on early, reliable indicators of movement. Signals that tend to appear quietly and gradually, often without announcement. These signals are easy to overlook if you are only watching for big moments.

Learning to recognise them changes how this phase feels. It replaces false stagnation with evidence of movement. It softens self-judgement. It restores trust in the process you are already in.

Progress does not disappear just because it is not yet visible. Sometimes it is simply happening beneath the surface, preparing the ground for what comes next.

Behavioural Signals

One of the earliest signs that something is shifting is behavioural.

Not dramatic action. Not bold moves. Just small, self-directed behaviour that wasn't there before.

During periods of stagnation or overwhelm, most action is reactive. You respond to demands, distractions, or worries as they arise. Choice feels limited, and initiative often disappears. When progress begins, that pattern starts to change quietly.

You may notice yourself taking action without being prompted. You do something because it feels appropriate, not because it is urgent or expected. There is no external deadline. No one is watching. The action happens anyway.

This matters more than it sounds. Initiative without pressure is a strong signal of agency returning. It suggests that your system no longer needs constant external cues to move. Even if the actions are small, the shift from reaction to choice is significant.

Another behavioural signal is the ability to complete small actions without spiralling. You start something. You finish it. You stop.

There may still be hesitation, but it no longer expands into overthinking, self-criticism, or avoidance. The action remains contained. This containment is progress.

You may also notice that decision-making feels slightly less fraught. Instead of delaying or deferring, you choose and move on. The choices themselves may be low-stakes, but the act of choosing is important. It indicates a growing tolerance for uncertainty and a reduced need for perfect information.

These behaviours are easy to dismiss because they feel ordinary. You might tell yourself that they "don't count", that they are too small, or that you should have been doing them all along. This is a mistake.

During transition, ordinary action is not ordinary. It is evidence. It shows that you are no longer frozen, even if you are not yet moving fast. It shows that momentum is beginning to rebuild from the inside out.

It can be helpful to notice the difference between effort driven by anxiety and effort driven by alignment.

Anxious effort feels compulsive and draining. Aligned effort feels quieter. It does not demand attention or applause. It simply happens.

If you find yourself acting more often from the second place than the first, something is changing.

You might recognise this in small ways:
- doing something without telling anyone
- choosing rest without guilt
- taking a step without rehearsing the outcome
- stopping when the action is complete

None of these behaviours guarantee results. They do something more important at this stage. They restore the experience of being able to act without force.

That experience is one of the clearest early signs that progress is already underway.

EMOTIONAL SIGNALS

Emotional change during transition is often subtle.

People expect progress to feel like confidence returning or fear disappearing. When that does not happen, they assume nothing has shifted. In reality, emotional progress usually shows up as less intensity, not sudden positivity.

One of the earliest emotional signals is reduced dread. Situations that once triggered a tight, anticipatory anxiety begin to feel more manageable. The fear may still be present, but it no longer dominates the experience. You can approach a decision, a conversation, or an unknown without the same sense of threat.

This matters. Reduced dread suggests that your nervous system is beginning to trust the environment again. You are no longer bracing for impact at every turn.

Another signal is a softening of self-judgement. The internal commentary that once felt harsh or relentless becomes quieter. You may still notice critical thoughts, but they do not carry the same authority. You are less inclined to treat every hesitation as a personal flaw.

This shift is easy to miss because it does not announce itself. You might simply notice that you recover more quickly. That a difficult day does not define the whole week. That a moment of doubt does not spiral into a verdict on your character or future.

Increased tolerance for ambiguity is another important emotional signal. Early in transition, uncertainty can feel unbearable. The absence of clear answers creates constant tension. As progress is made, that tension loosens slightly. You may still want clarity, but the lack of it feels less threatening.

You are able to hold questions without immediately needing to resolve them. This does not mean you enjoy uncertainty. It means you can live alongside it without being consumed by it.

It is important to be clear about what emotional progress does not look like.

It does not mean you are calm all the time. It does not mean fear is gone. It does not mean you feel confident or optimistic.

Emotional progress often looks like neutrality. Less reactivity. Less rumination. More space between thought and response.

These shifts can feel anticlimactic, especially if you are waiting for a dramatic emotional turnaround. But they are meaningful.

They indicate that your internal environment is becoming more stable, even if nothing external has changed yet.

If you find yourself thinking, "I'm not happy, but I'm not panicking either," that is not nothing. That is progress.

ENERGY SIGNALS

Energy is often one of the first things to disappear during periods of disruption.

Not physical energy necessarily, but the sense of engagement that makes things feel worth attending to. When work and identity are unsettled, many people describe feeling flat, numb, or indifferent. They may still function, but nothing seems to hold their attention for long.

When energy begins to return, it rarely does so dramatically. It shows up as curiosity before motivation. As interest before excitement. As attention that lingers just a little longer than it used to.

You may notice yourself pausing on an idea instead of scrolling past it. Reading a little further than expected. Thinking about something again later in the day. These are small signals, but they matter.

They indicate that engagement is re-emerging without force. This kind of energy does not announce itself with enthusiasm. In fact, it can feel almost neutral. You may not label it as energy at all. You may simply notice that something is pulling at your attention in a gentle way.

This is why it is often missed. People look for motivation and overlook curiosity. They wait for passion and ignore interest. In doing so, they miss one of the most reliable early indicators of progress.

Mild engagement replacing numbness is significant. It suggests that your system is no longer in pure conservation mode. You are beginning to invest attention again, even if only in small amounts. That investment creates the conditions for direction to form later.

It is important not to overburden these signals. Curiosity is fragile. If you immediately demand that it become a plan, a goal, or a justification for action, it often retreats. At this stage, it is enough to notice where energy appears and allow it to come and go.

You might recognise energy signals in moments like these:
- feeling interested rather than obligated
- wanting to understand something more deeply
- noticing time pass differently during an activity
- experiencing a quiet sense of "this matters", without knowing why

None of these moments require explanation. They are not commitments. They are not declarations of purpose. They are simply signs that aliveness is returning.

If you find yourself saying, "I'm not excited, but I am interested," that is a meaningful shift.

Energy often returns before clarity. Noticing it without demanding more is one of the kindest ways to support progress during this phase.

SOCIAL SIGNALS

Social behaviour often changes before circumstances do.

This can be surprising, because people tend to associate social ease with external success. They expect conversations to feel lighter after things have worked out. In practice, the opposite is often true.

As internal steadiness returns, social interactions begin to shift quietly.

One of the earliest social signals is reaching out without rehearsing. When uncertainty is high, people tend to script conversations in advance. They anticipate questions, prepare explanations, and monitor how they are coming across. This makes even casual contact feel effortful.

As progress is made, that need to rehearse softens. You may find yourself sending a message without overthinking it. Starting a conversation without a clear agenda. Responding more naturally, rather than strategically. This is not recklessness. It is a sign that self-consciousness is loosening its grip.

Another signal is talking about yourself without apology. Early in transition, people often feel the need to justify where they are. They explain gaps. They soften statements. They pre-empt judgement. Over time, as internal alignment improves, that impulse fades.

You may notice that you describe your situation more plainly. With fewer qualifiers. Less defensiveness. You are not trying to convince anyone. You are simply stating where you are.

This ease carries over into listening. When self-monitoring decreases, attention frees up. You become more present in conversation. Less focused on how you are being perceived, more engaged with what is actually being said.

This shift is subtle, but meaningful. Listening without constant self-reference is a strong indicator that identity threat has reduced. You no longer need the interaction to confirm your worth. You can simply participate.

It is worth noting that none of these social signals require positive outcomes. Conversations may still go nowhere. Messages may not lead to opportunities. Nothing external may change at all. That does not invalidate the signal.

The signal is the change in how it feels to engage. If conversations feel lighter, even briefly, something internal has stabilised. If you find yourself less preoccupied with impression management, progress is underway.

Social ease often precedes external opportunity, not the other way around. By the time outcomes appear, these shifts have usually been present for some time.

What Progress Doesn't Feel Like

One of the easiest ways to miss progress is to wait for it to feel a certain way.

People often assume that when things are improving, they will notice. That progress will arrive with relief, confidence, or a clear sense of momentum. When those feelings do not appear, they conclude that nothing has changed.

This assumption is misleading. Progress during transition is rarely dramatic. It does not announce itself. It often arrives quietly, without fanfare, and without changing the surface of your life in obvious ways.

It may feel anticlimactic. You may notice fewer spikes of anxiety, but no surge of confidence. You may feel slightly steadier, but not optimistic. You may be functioning better, but not happier. These shifts are easy to dismiss because they do not match the story we are told about what progress should feel like.

Progress may also feel invisible. Because it is internal at first, there is nothing to point to. No milestone to mark. No external confirmation to lean on. From the outside, and sometimes from the inside, it can look like nothing is happening.

This is where many people become discouraged. They look for resolution and do not find it. They look for certainty and find questions instead. They mistake the absence of dramatic change for failure.

It is important to be clear about what progress does not feel like at this stage. It does not necessarily feel like relief. It does not feel like confidence. It does not feel like clarity. It does not feel like momentum.

Waiting for those sensations can keep you stuck in a constant state of "not yet". What progress often feels like is neutrality. Less reactivity. Less dread. More space.

It may feel almost boring. You may go through a day without a spike of anxiety and barely register it. You may make a decision without overthinking and not think to celebrate it. You may notice curiosity flicker and fade without drawing conclusions.

These moments are easy to overlook, but they are meaningful. They indicate that your internal environment is becoming more stable. That you are no longer bracing constantly. That you are building capacity to move forward without forcing outcomes.

If you find yourself thinking, "Nothing has resolved, but things feel different," that is worth paying attention to.

Progress does not require resolution to be real. Something can be happening beneath the surface, preparing the ground for what comes next, even if you cannot yet see where it leads.

This chapter has focused on recognising those signals so you do not disqualify yourself too early. You are not meant to feel finished here. You are meant to feel steadier. That steadiness is often the clearest sign that progress is already underway.

Chapter 9

WHERE THIS LEADS NEXT

WHAT THIS TRANSITION HAS PREPARED YOU FOR

It may not feel like it, but something important has already shifted.

This book was not designed to move you quickly or decisively towards a particular outcome. It was not a productivity system, a career plan, or a set of instructions to follow. Its purpose was quieter than that. It was about restoring capacity.

Before clarity, before direction, and before outcomes, there needs to be a sense that you can act without panic, speak without apology, and engage without fear of being exposed or left behind. That is what this phase has been preparing you for.

You now have re-established agency. Not the kind that comes from knowing exactly what to do, but the kind that comes from being able to choose small actions without force. You have experienced yourself acting deliberately again, even when certainty was absent. That matters more than it might seem.

You also have a more flexible way of describing yourself. Instead of relying on fixed titles or outdated narratives, you have language that can move with you. You can speak about strengths, evidence, and interests without pretending the future is already settled. This makes engagement safer and more honest.

Perhaps most importantly, the fear around representation has softened. You no longer need to explain yourself perfectly or defend the shape of this phase. You can be seen without performing certainty. You can talk about where you are without treating it as a problem to solve.

These shifts may feel subtle. There may be no moment you can point to and say, "This is where it changed." But together they create a different internal landscape. One where movement is possible again, even if direction is still forming.

This is why it can be misleading to think of this work as unfinished. It was never meant to deliver answers. It was meant to prepare the ground. To restore steadiness, dignity, and trust in your ability to navigate what comes next when it arrives.

In that sense, you are not waiting to begin. You have already begun.

The sections that follow explore the different ways people often move from here, not as a set of steps to follow, but as a way of understanding what tends to come next when readiness has been quietly rebuilt.

For now, it is enough to recognise this: you are more able to move than you were when you started. That, in itself, is progress.

COMMON NEXT TRANSITIONS

There is no single direction that follows this phase.

Once steadiness returns and fear reduces, people tend to move in different ways, depending on their circumstances, energy, and priorities. What matters is not which transition comes next, but that movement, when it happens, feels chosen rather than forced.

It can be helpful to know what commonly emerges from this point, not as a map to follow, but as reassurance that there are many legitimate paths forward.

Moving Towards New Work

For some people, the next transition involves moving towards new employment.

This does not always look like a dramatic leap or a reinvention. Often, it is a quieter re-entry, approached with a different internal posture. There is less urgency to secure a role at any cost, and more attention paid to fit, values, and sustainability.

People who move this way often notice:
- they describe themselves in terms of capability rather than title
- they engage in conversations without desperation
- they tolerate uncertainty in the search process more easily

The external process may look similar to before, but the internal experience is different. Work is no longer being asked to repair identity. It is being asked to support it.

Reconfiguring Existing Work

Others discover that they do not need something entirely new.

Instead, they adjust the shape of what they already have. This might involve redefining responsibilities, setting firmer boundaries, changing emphasis, or renegotiating how work fits into life.

This kind of transition is often underestimated, but it can be significant.

Reconfiguration allows people to carry forward continuity while addressing what no longer fits. It is not about settling. It is about alignment.

For some, this is the most sustainable form of movement.

DESIGNING SOMETHING DIFFERENT ENTIRELY

Some people find themselves drawn towards something less defined.

This might include portfolio paths, independent work, creative projects, or experimentation that does not yet have a name. These transitions often begin tentatively, alongside other commitments, rather than as full declarations.

What distinguishes this path is not boldness, but curiosity.

People explore without demanding certainty. They test ideas without committing to identity. Over time, some experiments deepen. Others fall away. Both outcomes are valid.

This kind of movement is rarely linear, but it can be deeply formative.

STAYING HERE LONGER, DELIBERATELY

Finally, some people choose not to move on at all, at least not yet.

They remain in this phase intentionally, not because they are stuck, but because they recognise that more integration is needed. They allow insights to settle. They continue small actions without pushing for resolution.

This is not avoidance.

Deliberate stillness can be an active choice, especially after periods of pressure or acceleration. For some, staying here longer creates the conditions for clarity that could not be rushed.

No Hierarchy, No Schedule

None of these transitions are better than the others.

They do not follow a set order. They do not arrive on a timetable. Movement may be subtle or delayed. It may also change direction more than once.

What they have in common is that they tend to emerge once fear has eased and agency has returned.

Knowing this can reduce the pressure to decide.

You do not need to choose your path now. You only need to recognise that there are many ways forward, and that readiness often reveals itself gradually.

Timing Matters

One of the most unhelpful pressures people place on themselves during transition is the idea that there is a right time to move on.

Not just in the practical sense, but in a moral one. As though staying too long in uncertainty reflects a lack of discipline, courage, or ambition. This belief quietly turns timing into a judgement, rather than a consideration.

In reality, timing is personal. People pause for different reasons. Some need rest after long periods of intensity. Some need space to integrate what they have learned. Some are waiting for external circumstances to shift. None of these reasons are failures.

What often gets labelled as "being stuck" is simply being early. Early for clarity. Early for commitment. Early for resolution.

Forcing movement before readiness tends to create brittle decisions. People leap into roles or paths that quiet anxiety in the short term but recreate the same tensions later. In hindsight, they often recognise that what they needed was not acceleration, but time.

This is why pausing can be active rather than passive. An intentional pause allows signals to accumulate. It gives space for emotional reactivity to settle, for energy to return in usable ways, and for patterns to become clearer. These things are difficult to rush.

It is also important to distinguish between avoidance and stillness.

Avoidance feels tight and anxious. It is characterised by distraction, numbing, or constant postponement. Stillness, by contrast, feels steadier. It is chosen. It has edges. It does not require justification.

If you are acting in small ways, noticing signals, and remaining engaged with your life, you are not avoiding. You are integrating.

Comparison makes this harder. It is easy to look at others who appear to have moved on and conclude that you are behind. But you rarely see the full context of someone else's timing, the costs they may be carrying, or the compromises they have made.

Your pace does not need to match anyone else's. Readiness is not something you can argue yourself into. It emerges when enough internal conditions are in place. Until then, pressure tends to create noise rather than clarity.

It can help to remind yourself:

- This isn't avoidance, it's integration.
- I'm letting things settle.
- I don't need to rush clarity.

Timing is not a test. It is a variable.

How the Wider Work Fits

It can be tempting, at this point, to look for the next thing to follow.

Another book. Another framework. Another set of answers that might finally resolve what is still forming.

This chapter takes a lighter approach.

The work you have done here is not a step in a funnel. It is not designed to push you onwards. It is meant to sit alongside the rest of your life, supporting you while you regain steadiness and trust in your own judgement.

For some people, this phase is enough.

They move forward without consciously seeking anything else. The language settles. The fear continues to soften. Decisions begin to make themselves obvious through use rather than analysis.

For others, different ideas or perspectives become useful later. When people are ready, they often find themselves drawn towards work that deepens something already in motion. Not because they should, but because it resonates with a question they are now able to ask.

That might be:

- material that explores values and meaning more deeply
- work focused on building momentum or direction
- frameworks that support leadership, creativity, or contribution
- or reflections that help integrate change over time

None of this needs to happen now.

There is no implied progression here. No ladder to climb. No promise that the "next" thing will deliver certainty or speed. Different work supports different moments, and usefulness tends to reveal itself gradually.

It is also valid to engage with ideas selectively.

You do not need to adopt a system wholesale. You can take a phrase, a question, or a way of seeing, and leave the rest. Orientation does not require commitment.

If you notice curiosity towards something else, that may be an energy signal rather than an instruction. It is enough to acknowledge it and let it be.

Equally, if nothing else is calling to you, that is not a problem to solve.

You are not missing a step.

The purpose of this section is simply to place this work in context. To make it clear that it stands on its own, and that anything beyond it is optional and timing-dependent.

You are allowed to remain here.

Choice Without Obligation

One of the quieter outcomes of this phase is the return of choice.

Not choice in the sense of having all options available, but choice in how you relate to movement itself. You are no longer being pushed by fear or pulled by comparison. You have space to decide what fits, when it fits.

With that choice comes an important realisation. You do not owe momentum to anyone.

There is no external authority keeping score. No timeline you must justify. No requirement to demonstrate progress in ways that satisfy other people's expectations. The pressure to move often comes from internalised standards rather than real necessity.

Stillness, when chosen, can be active.

It can be a way of consolidating learning, restoring energy, or allowing clarity to form without force. It can be a deliberate stance rather than a default. The difference lies in agency, not in appearance.

Readiness is personal. It cannot be measured from the outside. It cannot be accelerated through argument or willpower. It arrives when enough internal conditions are in place, and not a moment before. This is why obligation is unhelpful here.

When people feel they should move, they often make choices that do not fit. They borrow certainty, adopt language that is premature, or commit to paths that quiet anxiety but undermine alignment. In contrast, when movement is chosen freely, it tends to be steadier and more sustainable.

You are allowed to wait. You are allowed to act. You are allowed to change your mind. None of these require explanation.

This chapter has not tried to tell you what comes next. It has tried to show you that whatever comes next does not need to be rushed, justified, or performed.

If you leave this chapter with one thing, let it be this: You are not behind. You are not failing. You are not late. You are in a phase that is doing quiet work.

The final chapter closes this book without asking you to do anything more. It simply reminds you that this transition will end, even if it does not feel like it yet, and that you are capable of taking the next small step when it does.

Chapter 10

A QUIET CLOSING

PROGRESS IS UNEVEN

It is worth saying this plainly. Progress does not move in a straight line. Even after periods of insight, steadiness, or relief, doubt can return. Energy can dip. Old questions can resurface. This does not mean that anything has gone wrong.

Forward and back is normal. Integration is not linear. It unfolds in waves. You may feel grounded one week and uncertain the next. You may recognise progress one day and question it the day after. These fluctuations are part of how change settles into the body and mind.

Doubt recurring does not undo the work. The shifts you have made do not disappear simply because uncertainty revisits you. What changes is not the absence of doubt, but your relationship to it. You recover more quickly. You take it less personally. You no longer treat it as evidence of failure.

This is easy to forget in the moment. When uncertainty returns, people often assume they are back at the beginning. They judge themselves for not "holding onto" progress, as though steadiness were something to maintain through effort. In reality, steadiness is something that returns on its own once the system remembers how.

Nothing has gone wrong. The fact that you can notice fluctuation at all is a sign that awareness has increased. Earlier, everything may have felt chaotic or overwhelming. Now, you can see the movement. You can recognise the pattern without being consumed by it.

Progress does not vanish when it quietens. It continues beneath the surface, reshaping how you respond, choose, and engage. Even when it is not visible, it is still doing its work.

If you find yourself wobbling after finishing this book, that is not a failure of the process. It is the process.

Clarity Comes After Movement

One of the ideas that runs quietly through this book is that clarity does not come first.

It is tempting to believe that if you could just understand yourself better, make sense of the past, or think things through one more time, the next step would become obvious. For many people, this belief keeps them waiting far longer than they need to.

Clarity is rarely predictive. It does not arrive as a complete picture before anything changes. More often, it appears in hindsight, after movement has already taken place. You look back and realise that something shifted long before you had language for it.

This book was not asking you to force action. It was inviting you into small forms of movement, some visible and some quiet. Taking a step. Pausing deliberately. Speaking differently about yourself. Allowing uncertainty without rushing to resolve it.

All of these count. Stillness has also been a form of action here. Choosing not to push. Allowing things to settle. Letting energy return at its own pace. These moments may not have looked like progress, but they were shaping the conditions for it.

Action reshapes narrative. As behaviour changes, the story you tell about yourself begins to loosen. Identity becomes less brittle. Possibility re-enters without being demanded. Over time, clarity follows this reshaping, not the other way around.

You may not be able to name what has changed yet. That does not mean nothing has changed. Understanding often arrives quietly, after the body and nervous system have adjusted to a new way of being. When it does, it tends to feel obvious rather than dramatic, as though it had been forming for some time.

Nothing in this process was wasted. Every pause, every small action, every moment of restraint contributed to a different internal environment. One that is more capable of holding what comes next without force.

THIS TRANSITION WILL END

It can sometimes feel as though a difficult phase might stretch on indefinitely. When there is no clear milestone or turning point, the uncertainty itself can become tiring. People begin to wonder whether this is simply how things are now, whether the transition has no ending at all.

Most transitions do not end that way. They close gradually. There is rarely a moment you can point to and say, "This is where it finished." Instead, the grip loosens slowly. The questions lose urgency. The emotional charge fades. One day, you realise you are no longer thinking about it in the same way.

You do not need to force that ending. Trying to manufacture closure often adds pressure rather than relief. It encourages premature decisions, neat stories that do not quite fit, or the sense that something must be resolved before you are allowed to move on.

In reality, transitions tend to end on their own. Even if it does not feel like it yet, this phase will shift. The uncertainty will soften. Attention will move elsewhere. What feels all-consuming now will eventually take up less space.

This is not something you need to manage. You do not have to decide when this transition ends. You do not have to mark it properly. You do not have to make sense of it all before you are allowed to leave it behind.

Life does not require a clean handover. Sometimes a transition simply fades, replaced by something else that gradually takes precedence. By the time you notice, you are already somewhere new.

If you are reading this and feeling impatient for that to happen, that is understandable. Wanting relief is human. But endings tend to arrive more reliably when they are not chased. For now, it is enough to let this be unfinished.

REASSURANCE

It is important to say this clearly. You are not broken. There is nothing fundamentally wrong with you because you are uncertain, tired, or between chapters. These experiences are not evidence of failure. They are part of being human during change.

You are not late. There is no universal timetable you have missed. No hidden standard you have failed to meet. Your life is unfolding at its own pace, shaped by circumstances, choices, and timing that cannot be reduced to comparison.

You are not uniquely bad at this. Transition is difficult precisely because it does not follow rules. Struggling with it does not mean you are doing it incorrectly. It means you are in it.

And you are capable of the next small step. Not because you have everything figured out, but because you have already taken steps without certainty. You have acted, paused, reflected, and adjusted. That capacity has not disappeared.

You do not need to prove this to anyone. You do not need to feel confident or ready all at once. You only need to trust that when the next small step presents itself, you will be able to take it. That has been true before. It remains true now. Nothing more is required in this moment.

A Soft Goodbye

There is nothing you need to do after finishing this book.

No exercise to complete. No plan to make. No insight to act on immediately. You can simply close it.

What matters will carry forward on its own. The steadiness you have been building does not require attention to remain present. It will show up quietly, in the way you think, choose, and respond over time.

You do not need to hold onto this moment. You do not need to remember everything you have read. You do not need to keep the ideas active. They will surface when they are useful and stay in the background when they are not.

This book was meant to accompany you for a short stretch, not to stay with you indefinitely. You can return to your life now.

Whatever comes next does not need to be forced or announced. The next small step will appear when it is ready, and you will recognise it when it does.

For now, it is enough to be where you are. Calmer. More grounded. Quietly capable. That is a good place to **stop**.

About the Author

Dave Cook, the one and only Yorkshire Cowboy, started out life as a software engineer in the space industry - a true computer nerd with no social skills.

Dave's career literally took off once he understood the real value of lifelong learning and began the development of his own transferable skill set. Ten years later, he stepped into his first C-level role and has never looked back.

With two decades of C-suite experience behind him, Dave now dedicates his time to helping others achieve their career goals through coaching, mentoring, and writing.

A lifelong fan of Westerns, Dave learned to ride in the USA. He is now lucky enough to have his own horses and gets to wear his Stetson most days. You have probably worked out where his 'ranch' is located.

www.YorkshireCowboy.com

Acknowledgments

I'd like to thank my wife, Nicola, who has always encouraged me to write a book. Her love and support remain invaluable.

I'd also like to acknowledge all my wonderful colleagues from across space and time without whom I would not have learned half as much. You continue to inspire me to always do better.

I'd also like to thank everyone who has found themselves between roles, contracts, or identities, and shared their experiences with honesty and trust. This book exists because of those conversations. I hope it reflects them with the care they deserve.

Also by Dave Cook

The Stoic Atheist: Reason, Resilience, and Meaning in a Godless Universe

The Next Step: Break Free From Career Stagnation And Start Moving Towards The Future You Want

Get Up & Go: The No-Nonsense Guide To Building Momentum & Achieving Your Goals

Power-Up: Game-Changing Techniques to Become the Most Effective Executive in the Room

Maximise Your Career Potential: Essential Skills for a More Successful Future

.

Work with the Yorkshire Cowboy

I offer a range of services designed to help individuals and teams unlock their full potential. These include one-to-one and group coaching tailored to career development, learning and development programmes focused on building essential skills, bespoke team training to enhance collaboration and performance, and engaging speaking sessions that inspire and motivate. Each service is customised to meet your unique needs and drive meaningful results.

If you're ready to take the next step in your career or elevate your team's performance, contact me at **dave@yorkshirecowboy.com** to discuss how I can help.